OSPREY AIRCRAFT OF THE ACES 113

V1 FLYING BOMB ACES

SERIES EDITOR: TONY HOLMES

OSPREY AIRCRAFT OF THE ACES 113

V1 FLYING BOMB ACES

Andrew Thomas

OSPREY
PUBLISHING

Front Cover
The RAF's first jet fighters entered service on 12 July 1944 when two Meteor Is were delivered to Spitfire-equipped No 616 'South Yorkshire' Sqn at Culmhead, in Somerset. The highly experienced Wg Cdr Andrew McDowall, who had 13 victories to his name, was appointed CO of the unit. Just over a week later No 616 Sqn moved with five Meteor Is to Manston, in Kent, from where it flew the first operational jet anti-V1 patrol on the 27th. In the event the jet patrolled uneventfully near Ashford. Seven more sorties were flown through the afternoon that led to several frustrations, including one pilot having his cannon jam behind a V1. Another, Flg Off 'Dixie' Dean, had to haul off his target as he was approaching the balloon barrage.

The number of jets assigned to No 616 Sqn increased in early August, resulting in more sorties being mounted by pairs of Meteor Is in daylight hours. However, although these led to more encounters with V1s, the first success still eluded them.

At 1545 hrs on 4 August 'Dixie' Dean was scrambled by the Biggin Hill controller to patrol over central Kent between Ashford and Robertsbridge. Flying Meteor I EE216/YQ-E, Dean established his patrol line at 4500 ft. Thirty minutes later he spotted a V1 near Tonbridge heading northwest at an altitude of 1000 ft. Dean immediately dived and increased his speed to more than 450 mph before lining up astern the pilotless aircraft. When he squeezed his trigger the Meteor I's quartet of cannon failed to fire – this was not the first time the jet's guns had failed! Undeterred, and realising that he had sufficient speed, Dean edged his jet close to the 'buzz bomb' and then gingerly flew alongside it. Later, 'Dixie' Dean described what happened next;

'I half expected the guns to jam because several other pilots had had that difficulty before me. Closing in to attack, I found my four 20 mm guns would not fire owing to a technical problem. I also knew that any sudden movement would upset the V1, so, when my guns failed, I already had a good idea what I should do. I then flew my Meteor alongside the "Diver" for approximately 20-30 seconds. Gradually, I manoeuvred my wingtip a few inches under the wing of the "Diver", then, pulling my aircraft sharply upwards, I turned the "Diver" over onto its back and sent it diving to earth approximately four miles south of Tonbridge. When I got back to base at Manston I found there was a small dent in my wingtip where I had hit the bomb. This was the only damage to the aircraft, which was serviceable again within a few hours. I was informed that the Royal Observer Corps had confirmed one "Diver" had crashed at the position given by me. This is the first pilotless aircraft to be destroyed by a jet-propelled aircraft.'

Within a few minutes Flg Off J K 'Jock' Rodger also brought down a V1, but using his cannon. The unit diarist excitedly wrote at the end of the day, 'The Squadron is now thrilled at the first two kills, and is ready for more'.

Patrols continued through to month-end using the few available Meteor Is, and by 31 August No 616 Sqn had claimed 11 and three shared V1s destroyed. Although no single Meteor I pilot became a V1 ace, they were the pioneers of jet combat in the RAF (*Cover artwork by Mark Postlethwaite*)

First published in Great Britain in 2013 by Osprey Publishing
Midland House, West Way, Botley, Oxford, OX2 0PH
43-01 21st Street, Suite 220B, Long Island City, NY, 11101, USA

E-mail; info@ospreypublishing.com

Osprey Publishing is part of the Osprey Group

A CIP catalogue record for this book is available from the British Library

ISBN: 978 1 78096 292 4
PDF e-book ISBN: 978 1 78096 293 1
e-Pub ISBN: 978 1 78096 294 8

Edited by Tony Holmes
Cover Artwork by Mark Postlethwaite
Aircraft Profiles by Chris Davey
Index by Alan Thatcher
Originated by PDQ Digital Media Solutions, UK
Printed in China through Asia Pacific Offset Limited

13 14 15 16 10 9 8 7 6 5 4 3 2 1

Osprey Publishing is supporting the Woodland Trust, the UK's leading woodland conservation charity, by funding the dedication of trees.

www.ospreypublishing.com

CONTENTS

'BUZZ BOMBS'

't was like chasing a ball of fire across the sky. It flashed past on our starboard side a few thousand feet away at the same height as we were flying. I quickly turned to port and chased it. It was going pretty fast, but I caught up with it and opened fire from astern. At first there was no effect, so I closed in another 100 yards and gave it another burst. Then I went closer still and pressed the button again. This time, there was a terrific flash and explosion and the whole thing fell down in a vertical dive into the sea. The whole show was over in about three minutes.'

Thus wrote Flt Lt John Musgrave in his combat report after landing at Manston in the early hours of Friday, 16 June 1944. With his navigator, Flt Sgt F W Samwell, he was flying a Mosquito VI of No 605 'County of Warwick' Sqn – a night intruder unit – over the English Channel when at 0040 hrs they had spotted a flying bomb. After a short chase Musgrave had shot it down into the sea about 20 miles off Dunkirk. He had just claimed the first of 12 'robot planes' (as the press initially dubbed the V1, although it was soon generally known as the 'Doodlebug') he would be credited with destroying, becoming a V1 ace on 5 July.

Musgrave became the first pilot to down a V1 by a mere five minutes, beating No 219 Sqn's Flt Lt 'Sailor' Parker and his navigator, WO Don Godfrey, who used their Mosquito XVII nightfighter to destroy the first of the six 'Doodlebugs' they would be credited with over the next two weeks. For Parker, a former air gunner who had been awarded a DSM whilst flying Fulmars from Malta with the Royal Navy, it was the first of his many combat claims. He had spotted what appeared to be a bright white light or flare 40 minutes after midnight, but could not close nearer than a thousand yards, 'so gave target a very short burst and no strikes observed, but target blew up'. Before dawn had broken two more 'robot planes' had been shot down by John Musgrave's colleagues in No 605 Sqn.

The first V1 to fall during the bombardment of England fell to the guns of Flt Lt John Musgrave (left) and his navigator Flt Sgt F W Samwell of No 605 Sqn. The pair eventually shot down 12 flying bombs (*No 605 Sqn via I Piper*)

An FZG 76 or Fieseler Fi 103, better known to the Germans as the *Vergeltungswaffe 1* or V1, is prepared for launch on its 'ski-jump' by members of *Flak-Regiment* 155 (W) (*via John Weal*)

THE REVENGE WEAPON UNLEASHED

The arrival of the first flying bombs in the skies of southern England was not, however, a surprise, as the development of these and other German secret weapons projects had been known to Allied intelligence for some time. Designed by Fieseler and designated the Fi 103, the flying bomb was given the cover designation FZG 76 by the Luftwaffe and christened V1 (*Vergeltungswaffe* 1, literally 'Reprisal Weapon 1', so named in response to the Allied bombing of cities in the Third Reich) by the German Propaganda Ministry.

Development of the weapon had followed a proposal to the German Air Ministry (RLM) in November 1939 for a remote-controlled aircraft capable of carrying a 1000 kg (2200 lb) warhead a distance of 500 km (310 miles). The project was conducted by pulse-jet manufacturer Argus until June 1942, when Fieseler was nominated as the prime contractor after proposals were submitted to the RLM's Technical Office. Development of what was now the Fi 103 took place under Luftwaffe supervision at its Karlshagen test centre. Glide tests of the vehicle, which was air-dropped from a Fw 200 Condor, began in October, followed by the first pulse-jet powered flight in December when the Fi 103 V7 was launched from a He 111.

Built of welded sheet steel with plywood wings, the Fi 103 was a pilotless aircraft powered by a simple Argus pulse-jet engine that pulsed 50 times per second, so producing the characteristic sound that resulted in the colloquial name 'buzz bomb'. Just over 25 ft long, with a wingspan of 17 ft 6 in, it was guided by an internal gyro-stabilised system that sent command signals to the flying controls. Once over its target the V1's engine would cut out, causing the bomb to nose over and dive into the ground, detonating its 1870 lb (850 kg) high explosive warhead.

Although capable of being employed from the air by a He 111, the V1 was more usually launched from a fixed site by means of a 'ski jump'. By late 1943 the building of large numbers of these, and associated storage facilities,

had been detected by Allied reconnaissance in the Pas de Calais area of northern France, and it was correctly surmised that they were connected with one of the secret weapons programmes. Operations generated to counter these secret long-range weapons were codenamed *Crossbow*, and included action against their research and development facilities as well as manufacturing sites. It also covered the launch sites, with those associated with the V1 being codenamed 'Noball'. The strategic potential of a campaign of bombardment by the V1 was recognised, and Allied bombers were diverted to attack launch infrastructure when located, as there was now sufficient evidence to link the 'ski jump' structures to the threat.

The first raid on a 'Noball' site was mounted on 5 November 1943 when a facility at Mimoyecques, near Calais, was hit by Mitchells from No 2 Group. These long-range weapon sites then featured regularly on the target lists for RAF and USAAF tactical bombers and fighter-bombers, although they were to prove difficult to knock out and dangerous to attack due to them being heavily defended. In response, the Germans swiftly developed prefabricated facilities, and these soon blossomed throughout the region. To the Allied High Command, with eyes firmly fixed on the coming invasion of France, it was a matter of when, not if, the weapon would be unleashed. In Germany, on 16 May, Field Marshal Wilhelm Keitel issued Hitler's Directive for Operation *Kirschkern* ('Cherry Stone') to commence the bombardment of England by long-range weapons. The Luftwaffe unit formed to employ the V1 operationally was designated *Flak-Regiment* 155 (W) in an effort to disguise its true purpose. The unit was commanded by veteran artillery officer Oberst Max Wachtel.

The Allied landings in Normandy on 6 June 1944 required a riposte from the Germans, and despite only ten of the 55 launch sites being ready, from 0330 hrs on 13 June ten flying bombs were launched. Although four of them malfunctioned, the remaining six headed towards London, their passing being noted by many who would shortly be chasing them. Among the latter was No 56 Sqn's CO, Sqn Ldr Archie Hall, soon to become a V1 ace;

'We were all rudely awakened at dawn by a strange noise, and to our startled eyes there suddenly appeared the first jet-propelled flying bomb. It was this country's introduction to this new horror, and it was an eerie sensation to see it.'

The appearance of the first flying bombs over Kent was also noted by No 96 Sqn, whose records for 14 June stated;

'Well, well, whatever will happen next? At 0415 hrs the air raid siren sounded, and this time the news came from Biggin Hill that the Hun was sending over pilotless aircraft of some sort – his secret weapon perhaps? About 15-20 of these aircraft operated in two waves, target presumably London. Flt Lt Mellersh was just coming in to land and saw one crossing the 'drome at 1500 ft going quite slowly and flashing a yellow light from the tail at 0500 hrs. "Chuff bombs" seems the best name for them.'

The first V1 to reach its target struck a railway bridge in Bethnal Green, where it killed six and injured 30 – the first of almost 24,000 casualties in England over the coming months. It was little wonder, therefore, that countering the V1s, which were codenamed 'Divers', immediately assumed the highest priority.

THE FIRST V1 ACE

Under the leadership of Air Marshal Sir Roderick Hill, the Air Defence of Great Britain (ADGB) had developed plans to meet the perceived threat. There were specific zones for engagement by guns on the coast firing proximity-fused shells, with fighters operating over the sea and inland zones backed up by a balloon barrage as a last resort around the capital, all being informed by reports from radar and the Observer Corps.

Fighter patrols were soon instigated, although it was evident that with the V1's speed of around 400 mph at 2000 ft only the RAF's latest fighters – the Tempest V and Griffon-engined Spitfire XIV – were capable of catching the flying bombs, and tactics were quickly developed. The units flying the latter type, Nos 91 and 322 (Dutch) Sqns, formed No 24 Wing at West Malling, in Kent, under the command of 14-victory ace Wg Cdr Bobby Oxspring. He noted in his autobiography;

The man charged with heading up the air defences against the V1 was the C–in–C ADGB, Air Marshal Sir Roderick Hill, who had himself been a successful pilot during World War 1 (*RAF Bentley Priory*)

'We found the ideal tactics for destroying the menacing missiles to be crucially governed by the range at which we fired. Rounds shot from 250 yards or more usually hit the flying control system of the craft, which would then dive into the ground still with an active warhead. Opening fire from a range of 150 yards or less almost always clobbered the warhead, which could severely damage the attacking fighter when it exploded. The best chances for success came when shooting from between 200 and 250 yards, as from this distance you were reasonably certain of exploding the warhead in the air without undue damage to your fighter. Not surprisingly, the quality of shooting by the squadrons deployed against the "Divers" improved to a very high standard.'

Also allocated to the 'Diver' task were the Tempest Vs of No 150 Wing (Nos 3 and 486 Sqns) at Newchurch, in Kent, under Wg Cdr 'Bea' Beamont. He was told by his AOC, Air Vice Marshal 'Dingbat' Saunders, 'I want you to be well placed between Eastbourne and North Foreland for the V1s'.

With the Mosquitoes having opened the battle against the V1, shortly after dawn on 16 June the two day fighter wings began anti-'Diver' patrols, shooting down 12 flying bombs during the course of the day as they evolved techniques for dealing with the missiles. They were effectively 'writing the book' as they went along. The first to claim a flying bomb by day was Flt Sgt Morrie Rose of No 3 Sqn, who, at 0750 hrs, despatched one in flames near Maidstone. He described to the press how 'this new Nazi terror weapon didn't deviate an inch as it came straight on towards me. The whole situation seemed crazy, almost unreal. I just fixed it in my sights and gave it a full burst with my guns. Fortunately the thing blew up in mid-air'.

Ninety minutes later, near Faversham, Wg Cdr Beamont and his wingman Flt Sgt Bob Cole had their first encounter with a V1. Beamont subsequently recalled;

'I missed completely with my first burst. Another short burst hit its port outer wing, and then with all the remaining ammunition a long burst hit it first on the fuselage, without immediate effect, and finally in the engine, after which it stopped and began to go down. The V1 slowed rapidly but remained on an even keel and, as I overtook it on the port side, I was able to get a quick look at its slim, pointed fuselage, high-mounted ram jet engine at the back and short stubby wings. I called in Bob Cole to finish it off, which he did with a well aimed burst, and it rolled over onto its back and dived into a field, exploding with a lot of flame and black smoke.'

Beamont had claimed the first of 31 V1s that he would destroy. One result of this combat was that the veteran ace ordered the guns on his aircraft to be harmonised at 300 yards.

Almost 250 missiles had been fired at London and Southampton on 16 June, and although there was a significant failure rate, 73 had reached the capital.

That night the Mosquitoes were again active, and among those who were successful was No 219 Sqn's CO, Wg Cdr Archie Boyd. A veteran nightfighter pilot, he told the author, 'My final claim was early on 17 June 1944 after we had returned to the UK and were on Mosquitoes. It was a flying bomb'. Also active were the Mosquitoes of No 96 Sqn,

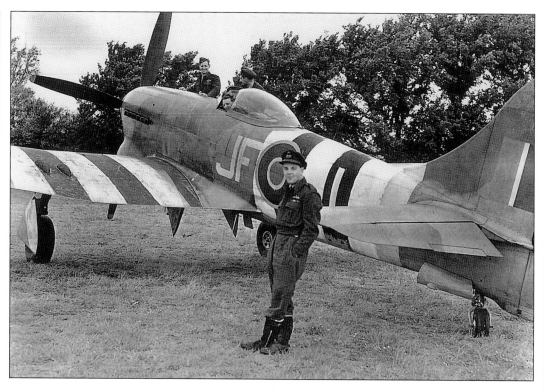

Leaning nonchalantly against the tailplane of a Tempest V of No 3 Sqn at Newchurch is Wg Cdr Roland 'Bea' Beamont, who was to become the first V1 ace. He would eventually shoot down 31 flying bombs, five of which were shared with other pilots (*P H T Green Collection*)

flying from Ford, in West Sussex. This unit would subsequently become the top scoring nightfighter unit during the V1 campaign, and fourth in the overall list, with between 165 and 174 victories. On the night of 17 June it claimed two, both being credited to future V1 aces Flt Lt Don Ward and Sqn Ldr Alastair Parker-Rees. The intruders of No 418 Sqn also got in on the act when, just after midnight, Flt Lt Don MacFadyen caught a 'Diver' off Dungeness and sent it into the sea on fire. The first of his five V1s was also the first to be brought down by the RCAF.

Dawn saw the barrage continue, with Beamont's Tempest wing very much to the fore. That afternoon and evening he shared another V1, whilst several of his pilots also began to score consistently, among them Belgian Flt Lt Remi van Lierde. It was on 18 June, however, that the day fighters really hit their stride, with No 3 Sqn bringing down 22, including three by New Zealander Flt Lt 'Spike' Umbers. His countrymen in No 486 Sqn destroyed 13, whilst between them the two Spitfire XIV units also claimed more than a dozen. Late in the evening 'Bea' Beamont blew one up over the sea and then shared another near Hastings to take his total to four. The following evening he was airborne again, and after being warned of a missile approaching Pevensey he watched the V1 being engaged by a Mustang without effect. Beamont then attacked. 'I fired a short burst from 250 yards and it went down on its back, diving into a wood two miles southwest of Tunbridge Wells'.

Beamont's fifth claim made him the first V1 ace, and more would reach this milestone within hours. By the end of the summer a further 154 pilots would have become V1 aces.

THE OPENING ROUNDS

ike the rest of No 150 Wing, No 486 Sqn began performing anti-'Diver' missions on 16 June. Tasked with flying a patrol line from Beachy Head to Folkestone, the unit claimed its first V1 when Flt Sgt Brian O'Connor intercepted a 'Diver' at midday at a height of 3000 ft near Hythe. Within a month O'Connor had become a V1 ace. Squadronmate and future V1 ace Plt Off Kevin McCarthy, in JN801/SA-L, shot down another near Rye soon afterwards.

The designated anti-V1 squadrons quickly reorganised their ops rota for the pilots, dividing each unit into two enlarged flights, each on standby for a 24-hour period. The defences were taking time to adjust, however, as No 486 Sqn's Flg Off Jack Stafford later recalled;

'My first flying bomb interception took place on 16 June. It was a total disaster. I caught up to the bomb, and while shooting my cannons jammed. I was then almost shot down by our own flak, which was totally disorganised and firing constantly, and badly, endangering our own fighters.'

By the end of July, however, the 22-year-old had shot down eight flying bombs, and Stafford later added five aircraft to his score too.

The opening rounds of the campaign against the V1 saw a swift reinforcement of units assigned to the task. However, there was also a natural eagerness by all fighter pilots to 'bag a Doodlebug', although their efforts were sometimes more in hope than expectation! The first of the reinforcement pilots to claim a V1 victory was the CO of No 142 Wing, 12-victory ace Wg Cdr Johnny Checketts. On 16 June he shot down a 'Diver' near Caterham, this success being all the more remarkable because Checketts was flying a Spitfire V.

Between them, No 486 Sqn pilots flying these Tempest Vs (JN754/SA-A and JN801/SA-L) from Newchurch shot down 24 V1s. Both fighters were flown by a number of 'Diver' aces, among them Flt Lt Harvey Sweetman, who claimed three in JN754 and two in JN801 (*RNZAF*)

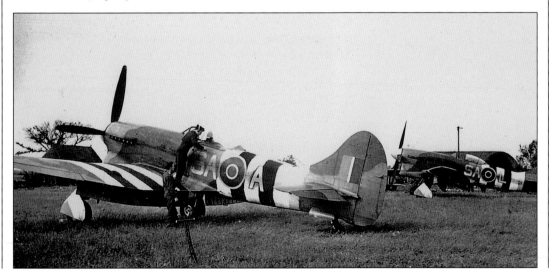

At midday on 16 June Flt Sgt Brian O'Connor shot down the first of almost 250 flying bombs that No 486 Sqn was to claim. He became a V1 ace on 11 July (*RNZAF*)

Destroying these unmanned aircraft was to be no sinecure, however, as was brutally brought home the next day when No 229 Sqn pilot Flt Lt Wally Iderma, an American in the RCAF, was killed when the V1 he was attacking exploded directly ahead of his Spitfire IX. He was the first of more than 70 pilots and navigators killed on anti-V1 operations over the next few months. The problems and hazards they faced were vividly described by Jack Stafford once again;

'Control was always totally accurate, and we would see the flak barrage that met the bomb and heralded its position. As soon as any of the missiles cleared the flak we would make our attack, starting with a long diving turn to bring us into the best position to engage. We would be at full revs and boost. The speed of our targets varied at times, but they would usually cross the Channel at around 350 mph. As they used up their fuel and became lighter, the "Divers" achieved speeds of around 400 mph. In our diving attacks, we would reach speeds of between 400-450 mph. This gave us two to three minutes to catch up with the flying bombs before they reached London.

'At a speed of around 430 mph the Tempest V was travelling through the air at something like 170 yards per second. You don't need to be Einstein to calculate that in the event of a bomb exploding the pilot has between one and two seconds to evade the blast, depending on the distance at which he opened fire. Consider also that the blast moved out in all directions – back towards the pursuing aircraft, as well as up and down. No wonder there were so many scorched Tempest Vs sitting around the airfield at times.'

Stafford's colleague WO Jimmy Sheddan added, 'It was frustrating to have a flying bomb leave you floundering in its wake as it headed towards London'.

THE CAMPAIGN WIDENS

As well as the dedicated anti-'Diver' units assigned to ADGB, airfields in the south of England were packed with RAF and USAAF fighters supporting the troops fighting in Normandy. Among the latter was the 354th Fighter Group (FG) at Lashenden, in Kent, whose pilots had seen the V1s flying above them in the night sky. Among the observers was future ace 1Lt William 'Swede' Anderson of the 356th Fighter Squadron (FS). At around 2000 hrs on 17 June he was returning to base after a ground-strafing sortie over France in his P-51B *Swede's Steed II* when he spotted a flying bomb and promptly shot it down. Anderson had just claimed the USAAF's first V1 kill, and after landing the 23-year-old excitedly asked 'How many "Doodlebugs" make an ace?'

A little later several of his squadronmates had some success too, including 1Lt Carl Bickel flying P-51B 43-6453/FT-Z *Z Hub*, who bagged three. He became an ace against aircraft in early July, shortly after the 354th had moved to France.

The Thunderbolt units also got in on the act during the evening of 17 June, with future seven-victory ace 1Lt Edwin 'Bill' Fisher of the 377th FS/362nd FG claiming a hat trick of V1s whilst at the controls of his personal P-47D 42-26918 *Shirley Jane III* (named after his wife).

Despite these successes – and a considerable haul claimed by the anti-aircraft artillery (AA) defences – flying bombs continued to explode all over southeast England, causing considerable damage and casualties. The night of the 17th was described by the No 96 Sqn diarist as, 'A foul night with limited flying, but the enemy used the pilotless aircraft bomb on quite a large scale for the first time'. The squadron's CO was Wg Cdr Edward Crew, who outlined to the author the problems presented from his perspective;

'The V1 was a small, fast target – it normally flew at about 2000 ft at 400 mph. To catch it in a Mosquito it was necessary to do a steep diving turn onto it, aiming to be within firing range at the bottom of the dive. The prospects of catching it in straight and level flight were not good. At night it was difficult to judge the range of the single exhaust flame, although at the optimum distance of about 100 yards it was possible to discern the red hot engine tube. If the warhead was hit the V1 blew up, and we inevitably flew through the explosion – one pilot reported a red-hot engine flying past him!

'In an attempt to improve the maximum speed of our aircraft, the Merlins were uprated to give a maximum of +25 lbs boost pressure, using 150 octane fuel. This led to a number of engine failures, one of which occurred when the uprated engine was being demonstrated to a Rolls-Royce representative!'

Nevertheless, Crew's squadron was highly successful, and he himself shot down 21 V1s. The first of these fell north of Dungeness at 0200 hrs on 21 June. Ninety minutes earlier Flt Lt Francis 'Togs' Mellersh (who had claimed seven victories over the Mediterranean, thus following in the

The first V1 to fall to the USAAF was shot down by 1Lt William 'Swede' Anderson of the 353rd FS/354th FG, who destroyed a missile whilst returning from Normandy. He later became an ace (*USAF*)

1Lt Anderson's squadronmate 1Lt Lewis H Powers also enjoyed success against the V1, downing 2.5 'Divers' in this P-51D during the evening of 17 June. This particular Mustang was usually flown by the CO of the 354th FG, 5.5-kill ace Col George Bickel (*USAF*)

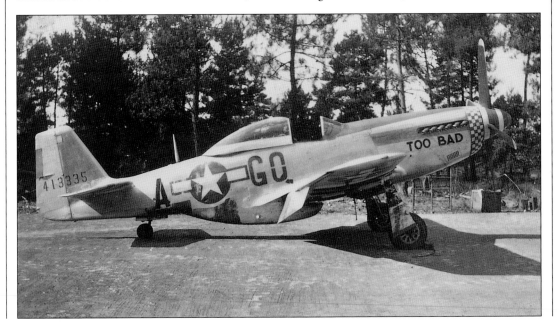

footsteps of his father who had become an ace in World War 1) had intercepted a V1 east of Dover. Closing in, he opened fire at a range of about 1000 ft and the 'Diver' crashed into the sea. This victory was the first of around 40 that he and his navigator, Flt Lt Michael Stanley, would be credited with over the next three months, making Mellersh the most successful nightfighter pilot against the V1, and third most successful pilot overall.

Four nights later, when over the Channel south of Hastings, an exploding flying bomb so damaged Crew's aircraft that he and his navigator had to bail out. That same night one of his pilots, Flg Off Norman Head, began his path to becoming a V1 ace whilst flying MM492/ZJ-C. He noted in his log book;

'Patrol. Exploded one flying bomb in air and forced to land at Manston. One engine dead, other half-dead. Both radiators punctured, perspex nose blown in and paint burnt off mainplane.'

By then Sqn Ldr Peter Green, a flight commander with No 96 Sqn, had become the first nightfighter V1 ace. He had claimed his two successes on the night of the 19th, and four days later had downed three more 'Divers' to become the first nightfighter V1 ace. Incredibly, such was the intensity of the offensive and pace of activity for the defenders that he was the 14th pilot to have claimed five V1s, with the campaign barely a week old! Almost all the others though had been flying the Tempest V, among them Kiwi Flt Lt 'Spike' Umbers and American Plt Off 'Buck' Feldman. Both were from No 3 Sqn, whilst No 486 Sqn's first V1 ace was Flt Lt Jim McCaw. He destroyed his first on the 19th, and by shooting down a hat trick on the morning of the 22nd achieved this ace distinction. Seen as something of an inspiration by his colleagues, McCaw subsequently inspired another generation when his grandson Richie captained the New Zealand rugby team to victory in the 2011 Rugby World Cup.

The leading nightfighter pilot against the V1, and the third ranking anti-'Diver' ace overall, was Flt Lt 'Togs' Mellersh, who also had eight victories against aircraft to his name (*author's collection*)

At night the defences initially relied on Mosquito nightfighters, including these Mk XIIIs of No 96 Sqn at West Malling. ZJ-B was flown by V1 ace Flt Lt Norman Head on occasion during July (*S Howe*)

15

It was on the evening of 18 June, however, that fellow Kiwi Flt Sgt Owen Eagleson, soon to be No 486 Sqn's leading scorer, engaged his first V1. It fell a few miles to the north of the unit's airstrip at Newchurch, and almost immediately Eagleson was vectored towards another to the north of Rye. His fire shredded its wings, and also accounted for a third V1 a few minutes later.

Whilst the bulk of the flying bombs shot down to date had fallen to Tempest Vs, the Spitfire XIV units, now joined by No 610 'County of Chester' Sqn, were also playing their part. In No 91 Sqn Flt Lt Paddy Schade, a successful Malta ace, shot down the first of 3.5 V1s he would be credited with, although he was to be killed the following month. Another No 91 Sqn pilot that began his path to V1 acedom at this time was Flg Off Ray McPhie, an experienced 22-year-old Canadian who, on 18 June, between Maidstone and Croydon shared in the destruction of two flying bombs and then shot down a third. He recalled the latter engagement many years later;

'I remember that before I shot it down I was flying side by side with the "Diver" because it was a relatively slow one. I had done an overshoot, but as I came up again it looked so ominous, a little bit small, ugly and a bit weird because there was no-one aboard. It was flying there full of explosives. You knew it was a bomb, but you didn't know what might blow it up. I whipped round and opened up with the 20 mm cannon.'

One of the leading New Zealand V1 aces was Flg Off Jim McCaw, whose grandson later led the All Blacks to win the Rugby World Cup in 2011 (*RNZAF*)

A happy WO Owen Eagleson of No 486 Sqn climbs out of Tempest V JN854/SA-G having shot down his eighth V1 on 28 June. On the ground are fellow 'Diver' aces Flg Off Kevin McCarthy (six), Flt Sgts Brian O'Connor (9.5) and Sid Short (four and two shared) (*RNZAF*)

The first V1 shot down by a Spitfire fell to a Mk XIV of No 91 Sqn on 16 June, and the first credited to RB188/ DL-K was claimed by Flt Sgt Kay three days later. The first V1 ace to destroy a 'Diver' with this aircraft was Flg Off Ken Collier, who claimed one on 22 June. Among other aces to enjoy success with this machine was Free French pilot Cne Jean-Marie Maridor (*Peter Hall*)

A quartet of Spitfire XIVs from No 610 Sqn fly over southern England in the summer of 1944. The nearest fighter is RB159/DW-D, which was the mount of Sqn Ldr R A Newbery. He made all of his V1 claims (eight and two shared destroyed) in this aircraft (*A P Ferguson*)

Sqn Ldr RA 'Dickie' Newbery of No 610 Sqn shot down ten V1s and four aircraft, thus narrowly missing becoming a 'dual' ace (*author's collection*)

McPhie noted in his log book his first encounter with the V1 – 'Lordy, what speed. Over 350 easily!' The CO of No 91 Sqn, Sqn Ldr Norman Kynaston, also destroyed two V1s on 18 June, one off Dungeness and the other that he chased down until it crashed near London.

The Dutchmen of No 322 Sqn also began scoring when Flg Off Rudi Burgwal brought a V1 down near Hastings on 18 June. Soon to be the most successful of the Dutch pilots, he wrote, 'Saw two "Divers" travelling inland over Hastings at 1000 ft. I attacked at 600 yards range. "Diver" exploded'.

The third Griffon-Spitfire unit, No 610 Sqn, began its contribution two days later when its CO, Sqn Ldr 'Dickie' Newbery, flying RB159/DW-D, shot a V1 down before lunch, writing, 'Under "Fairchild" control, sighted and chased a "Diver" on course 340 degrees, speed 320 mph, height 2500 ft. Opened fire 250 yards, jet exploded, bomb burst on ground'. He claimed a second in the evening. Ace Flt Lt John Shepherd, one of No 610 Sqn's flight commanders, also shot down a V1 at the same time for the first of his seven successes. It was Newbery, however, who in sharing a V1 on 23 June became the first of 33 Spitfire pilots to achieve acedom against the V1. And it was his squadron that also introduced modifications to improve the Spitfire XIV's already impressive performance. Higher grade 150 octane fuel was used and the engine boost increased from 18 to 21 inches, whilst the Browning guns were removed and plugged. Finally, the external rear view mirrors were removed and the aircraft surfaces highly polished, all to tease out a few more precious knots.

Also successful on the 23rd was Newbery's opposite number in No 322 Sqn, Maj Keith Kuhlmann, who at 2230 hrs downed his first V1. He claimed another five days later, stating in his combat report, 'Vectored onto "Diver" over Maidstone. Gave chase and fired three long bursts from dead astern. "Diver" turned over, righted itself, and then fell to the ground and exploded on a road or railway line in the Eynsford area'. Maj Kuhlmann was flying NH718/3W-G on both occasions, and he was the only SAAF pilot to claim the destruction of a flying bomb.

USAAF CONTRIBUTION

USAAF pilots also continued to play a small part in anti-'Diver' operations until their units' eventual move to France. Among them was eight-victory ace Maj Richard E Turner, the CO of Mustang-equipped 356th FS/354th FG. On the evening of 18 June he flew along the coast near Hastings looking for V1s, and at 2100 hrs he found one;

'I sighted one below and dived on it, pulling out behind it, but slightly out of range. I tried to close the distance, but the missile was just a little too fast. I chased the infernal machine for ten minutes, alternatively diving to gain speed and pulling up to lob long-range bursts at it. Eventually one of my bullets must have scored a chance hit in the engine, for suddenly it emitted a long streamer of yellow flame and quickly lost speed. In a curving dive, it plunged into a vacant field below, where the missile exploded harmlessly.

'Encouraged by my success, I proceeded back to the Channel area to pick up another. I began to wonder how I was going to get the next V1 because most of my ammo was expended and my gun barrels had burnt out. Soon I saw another one and made a very steep dive in order to gain extra overtaking speed. This bomb must have been moving more slowly than the first one, for I almost overran it as I pulled out of my dive. As I flew alongside the little monster, I had a new idea. I knew they were controlled by a gyro-guidance "brain", and perhaps this mechanism could be upset without gunfire. I carefully edged closer to it and placed my wingtip about a foot under its tiny fin. Rolling my aeroplane suddenly neatly flipped the V1 upside-down, and it promptly spun into the shallows of the Channel near the shoreline, where it blew a useless hole in the water. Jubilant with my success, I rushed back to Maidstone and hastened to tell the other pilots of the new pastime that I had discovered.'

The next day former RAF 'Eagle' pilot Capt Jim Dalglish of the 355th FS/354th FG, who already had four and two shared victories to his name, shot down the first of his three V1s. He noted;

'I was vectored onto a rocket in the Hastings area by "Snackbar". When I first saw it, I was at 6000 ft and the rocket at 1500 ft. I dove past two Spitfires and a Mustang, which were firing at it, and closed on the rocket, with an indicated speed of about 450 mph. The rocket was indicating 400 mph. I started firing from about 1000 yards but did not register hits until at about 400 yards. I scored hits on both wing roots and the rocket toppled to the right and went down in a descending turn, finally crashing in a wooded area near Penshurst. There was a lot of torque in its slipstream.'

As Dalglish had noted, however, coordination between pursuing fighters continued to be a problem, particularly with aircraft that were 'freelancing' rather than operating under ground control intercept radar control. This situation was highlighted to the author by Flt Lt Warren Peglar, who was flying Spitfire Vs with No 501 'County of Gloucester' Sqn;

No 91 Sqn's Flt Lt H D 'Johnny' Johnson shot down 3.5 of the 13.5 V1s he claimed when flying RB188, which was nicknamed *Brünhilde* and carried colourful nose art (*H D Johnson*)

A dramatic view of a Spitfire XIV edging in on a flying bomb prior to tipping it over with its port wing (*Royal Netherlands Air Force*)

The first pilot known to have downed a V1 by 'tipping' it over with his wingtip was Flg Off Ken Collier of No 91 Sqn, who achieved this feat on 23 June (*Peter Hall*)

'While on coastal patrol over the Dover area I was vectored onto a buzz-bomb headed for London. I caught up with it and, just as I was about to fire, a Tempest cut inside me and blew the wing off it. Down it went, exploding in a farmer's field.'

It was on 23 June that one of No 91 Sqn's Australian pilots, Flg Off Ken Collier, executed a cool act when on a 'Diver' patrol in Spitfire XIV NM698/DL-F. The squadron diary vividly described the novel method he used to destroy his target;

'He came across this particular "Diver" just after it had crossed over Beachy Head, and immediately gave chase. Getting within range, he fired, with no apparent effect as it carried straight on. This peeved him somewhat, so he had another go, and in fact several goes, but still nothing happened, and what was worse he ran clean out of ammo. By this time Ken was really swearing mad, and was determined to do or die. He therefore formated with it and with his wing tipped it over. On his second attempt, down it went in a tight spin, but it very nearly landed in the centre of East Grinstead. However, it did no damage, and Flg Off Collier thus brought into practice a new method of getting rid of these flying bombs.'

This was the second of Ken Collier's seven V1 kills.

As the number of V1s being launched by *Flak-Regiment* 155 (W) increased the campaign against London intensified, and their effects were terrifyingly indiscriminate. In one of the worst single incidents, on Sunday, 18 June, a V1 hit the Chapel at Wellington Barracks, killing

58 civilians and 63 servicemen. That evening future V1 ace Flt Sgt 'Artie' Shaw and Flt Sgt H C Drew of No 56 Sqn were flying Spitfire IXs on a weather reconnaissance mission when they fired at a V1. Later that same evening another V1 passed under the Spitfire IX of squadronmate Flt Lt Bateman-Jones, who quickly turned in behind it and fired a short burst at the 'Diver' from 300 yards astern. The flying bomb crashed in the sea near Hastings, thus giving No 56 Sqn its first 'Doodlebug' success.

It was also in a Merlin-engined Spitfire that Norwegian pilot Lt Ola Aanjesen, a future ace serving with No 332 Sqn, also brought a V1 down near Redhill, in Surrey.

To reinforce the defending day fighters Sqn Ldr M E Blackstone's Spitfire IX-equipped No 165 Sqn was moved up from Devon to Detling, in Kent. It quickly settled in and began 'Diver' patrols on 23 June, claiming six V1s later that evening. The first of these fell at 2045 hrs when Flt Lt Tony Holland brought one down near Rye. Five minutes later Australian Flg Off Tom Vance, who had six claims against aircraft, shot down one and shared another a little later. The CO also got in on the act, although his success again highlighted the problems of coordination amongst ADGB fighter units, as well as the Merlin-engined Spitfire's lack of performance when it came to chasing down V1s;

'I picked up the "Diver" on a northwesterly course over Beachy Head and gave chase with many other aircraft. After three minutes I was the only fighter left, but could not close. Indicated airspeed of the "Diver" was 375 mph at 2500-3000 ft. I chased it for about ten minutes until its "light" went out.'

As the flying bomb slowed, Blackstone managed to close and fire again, although without apparent effect. He persisted, trying to bring it down in open ground. The V1 eventually crashed on Wimbledon Common, and the report from the Royal Observer Corps resulted in Blackstone being credited with its destruction. At the same time, one of his pilots, Lt Selwyn Hamblett, brought another down near Hailsham to claim the first V1 kill by a Fleet Air Arm pilot in what was a very successful start for No 165 Sqn.

When the V1 offensive began one of the few Typhoon units remaining with ADGB was No 137 Sqn at Manston – a location that made it well placed to play a part in countering the menace, particularly as the Typhoon had a formidable low-level performance. The squadron was given clearance to begin anti-'Diver' missions when other tasks permitted on 22 June. That morning Plt Off Ken Brain shot down No 137 Sqn's first of 30 missile victories. Later that same morning Australian WO Jack Horne also spotted a V1 when returning from a shipping reconnaissance mission, and he tried a novel method against it;

'I saw a flying bomb coming out from France and I turned to chase it. The "Doodlebug" was doing about 380 mph, but I had a slight advantage in height, so I put the nose down, opened the throttle, put the pitch in fully fine and got after it. I opened fire at long range but I could see that the cannon shells were not hitting it and the range was getting greater. In desperation I raised the nose of the Typhoon and fired four pairs of rockets at it. At least one of the rockets hit the bomb because it started to break up and spun down into a field.'

The situation demanded that all methods of countering V1s be examined, as Jack Horne outlined after his unconventional use of 60-lb rocket projectiles;

'The following day a group captain from an experimental station arrived at Manston in a Mustang, which was equipped with rockets unlike any we'd seen before. They had Bakelite heads with a photo-electric cell that would trigger the 25-lb warhead if the rocket passed close to the "Doodlebug". The group captain told me that the rockets had originally been intended as a makeshift anti-aircraft defence earlier in the war. They loaded my aircraft up with similar rockets, which had been sent down by transport, and we both stooged up and down the Channel, but no flying bombs appeared that day.'

Also flying regularly with No 137 Sqn was Manston's Station Commander, Wg Cdr Gordon Raphael, who had been a successful nightfighter ace earlier in the war.

BY DAY AND NIGHT

With flying bombs continuing to crash into London around the clock, the night intruder squadrons played their part in anti-'Diver' operations. The exploits of Canadian-manned No 418 Sqn were particularly noteworthy. One of its pilots was American Flt Lt Merle Jasper, who was serving in the RCAF. He described the squadron's method of attacking a V1 during a press interview in which he also mentioned the risk of collision at night;

'We'd patrol at 8000 ft. The V1s would come over at about 3500 ft, cruising at about 350 mph. Control would vector you into the area when the V1s were spotted by coastal radar. If two or three Mosquitoes spotted the tail of fire at the same time, we would turn on our navigation lights so that we wouldn't run into each other. The pilot who was closest got the shot – the others would break off.

'At night, it was difficult to estimate your range accurately, although you had a rough idea. You saw the fire and just put your bead on it. Of course we dived on the V1s to get a speed advantage. If you tried to catch them in straight-and-level flight, they'd be over the coast before you could get within firing range. You didn't want to chase them over the coast where the balloon barrages and flak would take over.'

The reporter noted that by early July Jasper had downed three V1s. The American also outlined why they patrolled off the French coast;

'The missiles were most vulnerable over the Channel, when they were just beginning to accelerate. Although V1s could neither manoeuvre nor fire back, they could be dangerous if blown up at close range. This was demonstrated one night in late June when a Mosquito crewed by Flg Offs Sid Seid and Dave McIntosh, opened fire on a buzz bomb from a range of 50 ft. The blast that followed burned the paint from the fighter – even the roundels.'

Another of No 418 Sqn's pilots gave additional details of the unit's activities to the same journalist;

'We used to stooge around just out from the launching area in France. We were the first line nightfighter patrol. Sometimes we could see the actual launchings. A launching looks like a great half moon of brilliant explosion. Then when the thing came up it could be spotted by the steady glow from the rear end. Sometimes, from a distance, we weren't always sure whether there was a "Doodlebug" or not, so we used to line up the light with a star and then, if it moved, in we went.'

The same night (21/22 June) that Seid and McIntosh had their close call, Flt Off 'Bud' Miller, an NCO USAAF pilot in Mosquito-equipped No 605 Sqn, followed in the footsteps of his fellow American Merle Jasper by shooting down a V1. It was one of three destroyed by the squadron that night. He had scrambled from Manston, as the unit's Operations Record Book (ORB) laconically described;

'"Diver" sighted eight miles southeast of Le Touquet at 1400 ft doing 330 mph. Many short and one long burst fired from 600 yards. Finally target dived into the sea ten miles southeast of Eastbourne.'

Having taken his first step to becoming the only USAAF V1 ace, Miller was then transferred from No 605 Sqn to the Tempest Flight of the elite Fighter Interception Unit (FIU) at Newchurch to carry out experimental nightfighting work. The Ford-based FIU had received its first Tempest Vs for trials in night V1 interceptions earlier in the month, and on 24 June its CO, Wg Cdr C H Hartley, and Flt Lt Joe Berry flew a

Destroying more than 60 V1s, Flt Lt Joe Berry was the most successful anti-'Diver' pilot by some margin. Initially flying Tempest Vs with the FIU, he brought down his first missiles during the afternoon of 28 June. Promoted to the rank of squadron leader in early August, Berry commanded No 501 Sqn from the 16th of that month (*No 501 Sqn Association*)

pair of them to Newchurch – they were soon followed by seven-victory nightfighter ace Sqn Ldr Teddy Daniel and Flt Lt Jones.

It was Berry who gained the first success for the little detachment when, in poor weather during the afternoon of the 28th, he shot down two V1s – the first of no fewer than 60 that were to fall to his guns. Co-located with them at Newchurch, Wg Cdr 'Bea' Beamont of No 150 Wing had also been experimenting with night interceptions, describing one such sortie on 22 June;

'I took off for an experimental sortie from Newchurch and succeeded in intercepting and shooting down a V1 north of Hastings, but it was an imprecise and hazardous occupation at first.'

On 24 June No 486 Sqn's Plt Off Kevin McCarthy (who had claimed his fifth V1 the previous day) was flying JN803/SA-D when he had difficulty in closing in on his target;

'I tried raising the nose and taking a short burst, but by the time I got it right I was getting close to London. I saw strikes all over the flying bomb, and it started to dive. By then, however, I was so close to the balloon barrage that I had to turn away in a great hurry and I didn't see it hit the ground. On my next trip [1 July] I had engine failure over the sea at fairly low level. I couldn't bail out and had a pretty bad crash-landing, which put me in hospital for ten months.'

24 June had also seen Australian WO Richard 'Red' Blumer of No 91 Sqn killed when his Spitfire XIV crashed shortly after taking off on an anti-'Diver' sortie. With three and one shared aircraft destroyed to his name, Blumer seemed destined to 'make ace'. During the month of June the pilots of No 91 Sqn had destroyed 63 missiles, whilst their Dutch compatriots in No 322 Sqn had had their busiest day of the anti-V1 campaign on 29 June when they flew 62 sorties and destroyed ten flying bombs. The pace was maintained the next day when, just inland from Hastings, Rudi Burgwal shot down two – the first of these made him No 322 Sqn's premier V1 ace. He had attacked the flying bomb from the right, before moving to line astern at 300 yards and opening fire once again. He saw hits on its wings before the 'Diver' crashed into a small wood.

During a spell of poor weather at the end of June additional units were transferred in to join the anti-V1 campaign, particularly at night. One was the experienced No 157 Sqn, whose Mosquitoes moved down to West Malling on the 25th and began operations the next day, when its CO spotted three flying bombs – but only in the distance. The unit's first success came on the night of 27 June and fell to the ace crew of Flt Lts Ben Benson and Lewis Brandon. The latter graphically described the event;

'At 2255 hrs Ben and I found ourselves airborne on an anti-"Diver" patrol over the Somme Estuary. The weather was clear but dark, so we turned onto our northeasterly leg flying at 9000 ft. Suddenly it happened. Down there in the blackness we saw a moving light. It was followed in a matter of seconds by another and another, until within a minute there were five little lights below all heading northeast for London.'

After avoiding other nightfighters, they selected the third light as their target, but they failed to catch it. A little while later they spotted another barrage of missiles being launched, and again chased the third, eventually closing on their target as Lewis Brandon continued;

'I looked up as Ben pressed the gun button. We saw the tracer go slap into the flame. Flashes came from it as the shells struck home and the "Diver" was sent spinning into the sea. The strange flame from its tail was still burning until it hit the water.'

Also assigned to the campaign was the veteran No 85 Sqn under the command of Wg Cdr Charles Miller. Although the unit continued to fly its Mosquitoes from its Swannington, Norfolk, base, crews soon began knocking down V1s. Among the first to claim was seven-victory ace Flg Off Phillip Kendall, who brought one down on 27 June, while the following night future ace Flg Off Richard Goucher bagged another over the Channel.

As previously mentioned, earlier on 28 June the bad weather had meant that the FIU's Tempest V detachment was active in daytime, with Teddy Daniel and Joe Berry each flying three sorties – they opened their accounts by claiming two V1s apiece. These were the first for the detachment, although a few days earlier FIU aces Flt Lt Alan Wagner and Sqn Ldr Bill Maguire had each shot down a V1 flying a Mosquito. Joe Berry destroyed another the following night (29 June) and became a V1 ace in spectacular fashion on the night of the 30th when he shot down three. As June closed Berry was the 37th pilot to have become a V1 ace, with the campaign just two weeks old!

FLYING BOMB CLIMAX

The unseasonable wet and windy weather that had marked the end of June continued into July, although it had little impact on the intensity of the V1 campaign against southern England. In fact, the first week in July saw the assault reach its zenith. During a seven-day period more than 800 missiles were launched, and on Sunday, 2 July, no fewer than 161 were tracked crossing the south coast. This led Prime Minister Winston Churchill to later write that the V1 'imposed on the people of London a burden perhaps even heavier than the air raids of 1940 and 1941'. If anything, the weather helped the enemy, with low cloud shielding launch sites from Allied bombers and with higher cloud shielding the missiles in flight, particularly during daylight hours.

The indiscriminate nature of the attacks was highlighted on 1 July with the Colindale Hospital in north London being hit, killing ten. Then, shortly before midnight, another struck a residential area in Lambeth, killing 13.

On 1 July the flying bomb attacked by Flg Off G P Armstrong of No 165 Sqn blew up in front of him. Here, he ruefully surveys the damage to his fighter, Spitfire IX MJ221/SK-J, after landing. The narrow Allied Expeditionary Air Forces stripes worn by No 165 Sqn aircraft are noteworthy (*Charles Young*)

Flg Off Tommy Tinsey (centre) was one of No 165 Sqn's three V1 aces. The other two pilots are Plt Off Scott (left), who shot down four V1s, and Flt Lt A D May (*author's collection*)

The battered wing of a V1 was used as a scoreboard for Brenzett-based No 129 Sqn, which was the 'Mysore' gift squadron (*via W Matusiak*)

The day fighters naturally took a significant toll of the V1s during the daylight hours on the 1st, with most kills being achieved in the evening. Amongst the successful pilots was WO Jimmy Sheddan of No 486 Sqn, the missile he shared with a Spitfire a little after 1900 hrs making him a V1 ace. Also taking a significant step to achieving this distinction were No 165 Sqn's Flg Off 'Ac' Lawson, who shot down a brace over the coast a little after 1800 hrs (his first one exploding in the air), and Flg Off Tommy Tinsey, who had previously claimed victories over the Channel and North Africa. He shot down two V1s near Eastbourne later in the evening. Tinsey wrote of his second engagement that having flown past another Spitfire 'I opened fire from 100 yards. Gave one one-second burst. Large flash and large piece of jet unit fell away. "Diver" fell three miles southeast of Kenley'.

During the day the defenders were further reinforced when a flight from Sqn Ldr Bohdan Arct's Polish-manned No 316 Sqn, which had recently converted to the Mustang III, arrived at West Malling. Over the next two months the flight would shoot down 74 flying bombs to become the leading Polish squadron, although they were 'pipped' by No 129 Sqn for the title of the RAF's most successful Mustang III unit during the anti-'Diver' campaign.

In order to try and boost the American fighter's speed RAF units experimented with 130 octane fuel, although with mixed results.

No 316 Sqn's first V1 fell to Flt Sgt Toni Murkowski on 3 July, and he recounted the event to the author many years later;

'Because they were such small targets, our guns were harmonised for a range of about 260 yards. I remember my first one. It was a foggy day, and most of the pilots had gone to the Officers' Mess for lunch when the tannoy went and I scrambled to intercept a flying bomb coming in over Rye. It took some catching, and we were supposed to keep the over boost revs on for less than ten minutes or it meant an engine change. I soon saw it and opened fire, but I was too precise – and enthusiastic. I never got such a shock in the air as when I hit it and the V1 went up with a terrific explosion. This first one just blew up in front of me. My God, I never thought the Mustang would stand

the shock, the fighter being hit by pieces of the V1, while its left wing flew off above me. When I got back my wingtips had to be changed.'

Also returning to the fray, having swiftly converted to the Tempest V, was No 56 Sqn, whose first success fell to Flt Lt 'Digger' Cotes-Preedy (who earlier in the war had been awarded the George Medal) on 3 July shortly before Toni Murkowski had opened No 316 Sqn's 'book'. One of No 56 Sqn's Canadians, Plt Off David Ness, was less successful, however, as having used up all his ammunition he then tried three times to turn the V1 over with his wingtip. He brought down his first soon afterwards, thus beginning his path to V1 acedom.

In the prevailing bad weather the FIU Tempest V detachment had also been active, Flt Lt Joe Berry attacking a missile that exploded on 2 July. Debris struck his fighter, although he managed to coax the damaged aircraft back to Newchurch.

No 1 Sqn's most successful anti-V1 pilot opened his score two days later when Flg Off Dennis Davy, in Spitfire IX MK846, shot down his first 'Diver' near Hastings. His roommate was Flg Off Jack Batchelor, who recalled that Davy was 'a great chap. While I was on a 48-hour leave he shot down five V1s. We were all envious, and he was soon known as "ace Davy"'.

4 July also saw No 3 Sqn achieve its best results to date, claiming 14 V1s destroyed – four of these were credited to the unit's Belgian pilot Flt Lt Remi van Lierde in a single sortie. Then, in bringing down five in two sorties on the 5th, Flg Off Rod Dryland not only took his squadron's total past the 150 mark, but also elevated himself to V1 ace status. He reported afterwards how he achieved this distinction;

'I fired from 150 yards and blew the port wing off the "Diver", which exploded when it hit the ground one mile north of Rye. Saw second "Diver" eight miles north of Dungeness at 3500 ft. Closed to 100 yards

The second most successful pilot in the V1 campaign was Flt Lt Remi van Lierde of No 3 Sqn, who claimed no fewer than 36 missiles destroyed in Tempest V JN862/JF-Z (O G Thetford)

Flt Lt Remi van Lierde, seen here meeting Gen Dwight D Eisenhower, was one of the leading Belgian pilots of World War 2, having first seen action flying antiquated Fairey Foxes in 1940! (*via C H Thomas*)

and gave it a short burst from astern, seeing strikes on the jet engine and wing. The jet engine went out and the "Diver" exploded on the ground. Saw a third five miles south of Beachy Head at 2000 ft and attacked with a short burst from 150 yards. Strikes were seen and the "Diver" went down, exploding on the ground east of Falmer.'

Also putting his name onto the V1 score list on 5 July was nine-victory ace and Detling Wing Leader Wg Cdr Peter Powell who, in his Spitfire IX, shot down two. His opposite number in No 150 Wing, Wg Cdr 'Bea' Beamont, was also in action when he shared a V1 with No 486 Sqn's WO Jimmy Sheddan. The latter, who had become a V1 ace on 1 July, vividly described the hazards of chasing the same target;

'I had just scored numerous hits on a "Diver", and was watching as it headed towards the ground, when in front of me there appeared another Tempest. The smoke drifting back from the front of the wings indicated that the pilot was shooting at my wounded bird. As the flying bomb increased its angle of dive I ranged up alongside the Tempest and watched as the marksman continued to fire, without any visible strikes. Then "Bang!" My engine suddenly ground to a stop, and with it the propeller.'

Sheddan was forced into a high-speed crash landing that he was fortunate to survive with only minor injuries – he was hospitalised for several weeks. It transpired that a shell casing from Beamont's fire had lodged in the intake of Sheddan's fighter, causing the engine to seize.

The FIU's small detachment was also in action on 5 July, and Joe Berry bagged a pair. Tragically, however, the missile that detachment commander Sqn Ldr Teddy Daniel attacked exploded directly in front of him, stopping the engine of his Tempest V. Although Daniel managed to bail out over the Channel, he was not found, and so became the first ace to perish in the V1 campaign.

Spitfire XIV NH654 of No 91 Sqn sits awaiting its next sortie at Deanland in July. Free French pilot Cne Jean-Marie Maridor shot down his penultimate V1 in this machine on 5 July (R S Nash)

Those flying at night were continuing to reap their nocturnal harvest of V1s too, for the campaign effort truly went on round the clock. On the night of 5/6 July, for example, the Mosquito crews of No 96 Sqn knocked down eight, with 'Togs' Mellersh and Sqn Ldr Alastair Parker-Rees each claiming two. Their CO, Wg Cdr Edward Crew, went one better, thus emulating his feat of three nights earlier. Also successful on the night of the 5/6 July was Flt Lt John Musgrave, who, having been credited with bringing down the first flying bomb barely three weeks earlier, was on patrol off the French coast at Le Touquet when he shot down two to become the 42nd V1 ace!

Musgrave had taken off from Manston in his Mosquito VI in the early hours of 6 July, and shortly after 0200 hrs he saw eight flying bombs being launched. Diving on one, he opened fire with his cannon and the V1 exploded in mid-air. Musgrave then destroyed a second flying bomb with an identical attack. Following several inconclusive attacks over the next hour, he intercepted another 'Diver' at 3000 ft mid-Channel and probably destroyed it.

Earlier that same night Musgrave's Station Commander at Manston, Wg Cdr Gordon Raphael, flying a Typhoon from No 137 Sqn, shot down another V1. Other pilots from this Typhoon squadron were also active on 5/6 July, with Flg Offs Henry Nicholls and Jim Holder patrolling the Channel as Yellow Section. The latter shot a V1 down off Dungeness to claim the first of his four missiles, whilst 45 minutes later his section leader spotted the engine flame of another off the port of Boulogne;

'I dived onto it, attacking from above and astern with a one-second burst from 100 yards. It dived into the sea and exploded. I then chased and attacked a second one from astern from 500 yards. Target dived into the sea and a splash was seen.'

Holder claimed a third flying bomb a few days later. Nicholls had achieved acedom flying Hurricanes over Malaya in the doomed campaign against the Japanese in 1942, being one of the fortunate few to have escaped captivity.

Pilots flying Typhoon IB MN134/ SF-S of No 137 Sqn from Manston shot down no fewer than 11.5 V1s. Among them were 'Diver' ace Flg Off 'Artie' Sames and aces Flg Off Henry Nicholls and Wg Cdr Gordon Raphael (*via C H Thomas*)

With 18.5 V1s destroyed, Sqn Ldr Russ Bannock (left) and his navigator Flg Off Robert Bruce of No 418 Sqn were one of the top Mosquito crews in 1944. Their V1 victories were all achieved in Mosquito VI HK147/TH-Z, which was nicknamed *Hairless Joe*. Bannock later commanded No 406 Sqn, and made the last claim against a He 111 V1 carrier (*RCAF*)

ADGB Enlarged

Despite the efforts of the defences, the increasing damage and casualty lists caused by those V1s that reached London were starting to have a detrimental effect on civilian morale in the capital. In an effort to boost ADGB ranks, further squadrons in the form of the Mustang IIIs of No 133 Wing (Nos 129, 306 and 315 Sqns) were allocated to anti-'Diver' duties. They began operations a few days later.

The Tempest Vs of No 150 Wing remained in the vanguard of the aerial defences, bringing down 15 V1s on 6 July for example. That night No 96 Sqn destroyed seven more, but the high-scoring honours went to No 418 Sqn, whose Mosquito VI crews downed 12. Flt Lt Don McFadyen claimed three and Sqn Ldr Russ Bannock four, giving them V1 ace status in spectacular fashion. Bannock's fifth success was actually his first victory of the night, the Canadian attacking the flying bomb at an altitude of 3500 ft. Opening fire from astern with a one-and-a-half second burst from 400 yards, he saw the missile explode in the sea to the south of Beachy Head. Bannock later wrote, 'At least 40 V1s were launched during my two-hour patrol, but I ran out of ammo after downing the fourth bomb'.

Also achieving acedom that night was squadronmate Flt Lt Colin Evans, who, having destroyed one, then blew up a second V1. However, debris hit his Mosquito on this occasion, damaging its starboard engine. Nevertheless, Evans gamely continued flying on one engine, diving on a third V1 and shooting it down! Debris also damaged the FIU Tempest V of Flt Lt Joe Berry that night too, but not before he had destroyed four more 'Divers'. He managed to nurse his ailing fighter back to Newchurch.

With the dawn came the turn of the day fighters, with No 91 Sqn's Spitfire XIVs being particularly successful on 7 July, bringing down 12 V1s. The first was credited to Flt Lt Ray Nash over Dartford during an early morning patrol, this victory taking his tally to 12. Also in action was his CO, Sqn Ldr Norman Kynaston, who shot one down during each of the two sorties he flew that day. By month-end his tally would stand at 22. Their Dutch compatriots in No 322 Sqn were also active, bringing down six V1s.

There was relatively little activity during daylight hours on 8 July, but late that evening another barrage was launched and the Spitfire XIVs were heavily involved – not least 14-victory ace Wg Cdr Bobby Oxspring, the No 24 Wing Leader, who shot down two with his personal aircraft NH714, which bore his initials 'RWO'. However, it was Dutchman Flg Off Rudi Burgwal who had the day's most notable sortie when, near Rye, in little more than 90 minutes from 2130 hrs he shot down five V1s – the first pilot to achieve this feat thus far during the anti-'Diver' campaign. Also successful were his colleagues, and future V1 aces, Flt Lt Cees van Eendenborg and Flg Off Jan Jonker.

The Czech-manned Spitfire IX unit No 312 Sqn also got in on the act when Flg Off Otto Smik, a ten-victory ace, was on a 'Diver' patrol. One of his colleagues recalled that he 'had taken off at 2135 hrs and actually spotted the first V1 just three minutes later. Flg Off Smik attacked and destroyed it near Ashford, in Kent. Heading southwest, he then spotted another coming in over the Sussex coast, which he also destroyed. He downed his third flying bomb near Tenterden, Kent, at 2200 hrs'. Otto Smik received a bar to his DFC for this exploit.

Two of No 91 Sqn's V1 aces debrief after another sortie. On the left is Flg Off Ted Topham, who claimed 9.5 flying bombs, with Flt Lt Ray Nash (17 and three shared) in the centre and squadron intelligence officer Flg Off Kember to right (*R S Nash*)

The most successful pilot of No 322 (Dutch) Sqn with 20 and four shared V1s destroyed was Flg Off Rudi Burgwal. Sadly, he was killed over the Continent on 12 August, just days after No 322 Sqn's commitment to the anti-V1 campaign had ended (*P H T Green Collection*)

Flt Lt Norman Head of No 96 Sqn became a V1 ace on the night of 8 July when, flying a Mosquito XIII, he shot down his fifth V1. He was another pilot who narrowly missed out on being a double ace, claiming four destroyed and two probables against aircraft (*N S Head*)

Late on the evening of 8 July Burgwal flew one of the outstanding sorties of the entire campaign when, flying this Spitfire XIV (NH718/3W-G), he shot down five V1s in barely 40 minutes. The aircraft was the usual mount of his CO, Maj Keith Kuhlmann, who shot down two V1s in it to become the only SAAF pilot to claim 'Diver' kills (*M Schoemann*)

Also joining the spree of multiple claims on 8 July were No 486 Sqn's New Zealanders, with Flt Lt Jim McCaw downing four between 2300 hrs and midnight. The last of these exploded when it hit the ground at Biggin Hill. His wingman, Plt Off Bruce Lawless, bagged two more, taking his total to seven.

The more specialised nightfighters also got in on the act during 8/9 July, with No 96 Sqn's Mosquito crews shooting down nine – no fewer than six of them by one crew on two sorties! Sqn Ldr Dick Chudleigh and his navigator Flg Off D Ayliffe had previously shot down three on the night of 3 July, and so became a V1 ace crew in spectacular style. Also successful was Flg Off Norman Head, who, flying MM462/ZJ-E with Flg Off Andrews, shot down another to become an ace on 8/9 July, noting in his log book 'flak heavy from sites'. The following night his flight commander, Sqn Ldr Alastair Parker-Rees, achieved the same distinction, whilst No 219 Sqn claimed its final V1s near Broadstairs on 9/10 July, as its Mediterranean nightfighter ace Flt Lt Peter Williamson described;

'Was freelancing in the Straits area and had two combats with "Divers", the first at 2000 ft. Opened fire from 600 ft, strikes and explosions seen and target crashed on land. The second was further east at 3000 ft. Opened fire from 1000 ft, strikes seen and "Diver" nose-dived into sea 30 miles east of North Foreland.'

These successes took the unit's total to 20.

It was the evening patrols that continued to be busy, with No 91 Sqn's Flg Off John Draper causing much consternation to those on the ground by chasing a 'Diver' at low level over West Malling while blazing away with his cannon! Nonetheless, he claimed his fourth flying bomb, and within a few days had also become a V1 ace. No 310 Sqn's Flt Sgt Franticek Mares, who had five claims, including four destroyed, gave a vivid description in his autobiography of an evening sortie he flew on 9 July;

'The night was dark. After some 20 minutes of precise guidance the voice, calm and firm, announced "I have a 'Witch-craft' for you at '11 o'clock below'". No sooner had I received the message than I saw the flame of a V1 flying bomb racing towards me.'

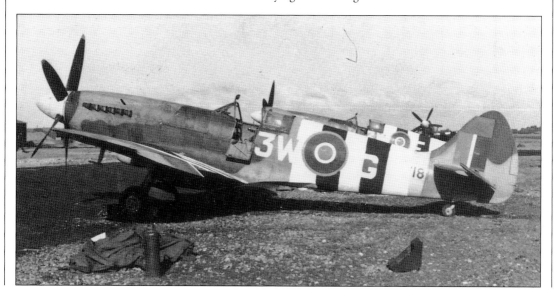

However, the engine of Mares' Spitfire IX then began 'coughing' at the critical moment! He continued;

'Just as I began to despair the engine regained its senses, roared into life and I was able to continue with the pursuit of the distant "Witch-craft" flame. With both man and machine revitalised, and the cannons spitting out their venom, I willed the shells towards their target. Just as I was declaring my mission a failure, there was a blinding flash and a terrific explosion, which preceded some very severe turbulence. My feeling was one of gleeful satisfaction.'

It was an explosion such as he described that probably caused the loss of one of No 610 Sqn's aircraft that night, however, when Flt Sgt Ingvar Håkansson, one of the few Swedish volunteer pilots in the RAF, was on patrol over the Channel in his Spitfire XIV. At about 0440 hrs he managed to destroy a pair of V1s, but his engine then cut, probably due to debris. Forced to bail out, Håkansson was not recovered from the sea. Later that same day (9 July) Flt Lt Stefan Karnkowski of No 316 Sqn became the first Polish V1 ace. He was also the first to achieve this feat in a Mustang III, although details of some of his claims remain unclear.

The night of 9/10 July also saw the Australian-manned No 456 Sqn finally claim its first 'Diver' destroyed after a series of frustrated attempts earlier that month. Future V1 ace Flt Lt Keith Roediger and his navigator Flt Lt Bob Dobson, in Mosquito XVII HK297, found one flying northwest at 2500 ft. Closing to 500 yards, and offsetting to the right, Roediger opened fire and sent the flying bomb crashing into the sea. Another was shot down the following night as No 456 Sqn got into its stride. Flt Lt Houston destroyed a third V1 on the 11th, but that these operations were no sinecure was brutally brought home in the early hours of 12 July when HK312/RX-G crashed off Littlehampton with the loss of Flg Off Ted Bradford and Flt Sgt Wally Atkinson. Based at Ford, the squadron's regular 'beat' was the line from Beachy Head to Bognor Regis.

V1s were engaged whenever they were encountered, including by No 277 Sqn, which was an air-sea rescue unit based at Shoreham. The squadron brought down five 'Divers' during the summer of 1944, including two credited to Wg Cdr A D Grace. No 277 Sqn's Spitfire VB BL591/BA-U is seen here at Shoreham in July 1944, with a Sea Otter amphibian from the unit parked behind it (*W A Rance*)

In early June the Mustang IIIs of No 129 Sqn that formed part of No 131 (Polish) Wing were thrown into the fight against the V1. One of its aircraft was FB125/DV-F, and amongst the pilots who claimed a V1 in it was the leading 'Diver' ace on the type, Flg Off Jim Hartley (*Paul Hamlin*)

The early morning of 10 July also saw a claim credited to a more unusual type. Flying from Hawkinge on a 'Channel Stop' operation, a Royal Navy Avenger of 854 Naval Air Squadron, flown by Sub Lt D P Davies, was at the end of a long patrol when at 0510 hrs Telegraphist Air Gunner L/A Fred Shirmer spotted a V1 approaching from behind. The 'Diver' gradually overtook them, and as the flying bomb passed about 700 yards down the port side Shirmer fired on it with his turret-mounted 0.50-in machine gun. His aim was good, for although he only fired 20 rounds, the V1 went down. This was the first time a flying bomb had been destroyed by a Fleet Air Arm aircraft, and it resulted in Shirmer subsequently being Mentioned in Despatches.

Having moved into Brenzett, Kent, Mustang III-equipped Nos 129 and 306 Sqns also began ADGB operations following their withdrawal from 2nd TAF. They were joined at the airfield by No 315 Sqn, led by the charismatic Sqn Ldr Eugeniusz Horbaczewski. This trio of Mustang III squadrons swiftly opened their accounts when, shortly after noon on 10 July, future V1 ace Flt Sgt Stanislaw Rudowski shot a flying bomb down near Kenley. No 129 Sqn claimed its first flying bomb that evening, with No 315 Sqn following suit the following afternoon when Flt Sgt Tadeusz Jankowski set out on the road to becoming a V1 ace. Several hours later No 129 Sqn's Flg Off Jim Hartley blew up a V1 over Folkestone – the first of 12 'Divers' he was to destroy to become the leading Mustang III V1 ace.

Just 25 minutes before Hartley's success, at 2050 hrs, Flt Sgt Iain Hastings of No 1 Sqn, at the controls of Spitfire IX ML117, attacked a missile north of Hastings until he was baulked by another Spitfire;

'Fired burst of two seconds. On second burst, while still firing, a XIV came in front from "one o'clock above". Pushed nose down to save hitting XIV. Saw strikes on port wing. While XIV was still firing, the "Diver" blew up and both of us flew through it.'

Although only credited with a share in the V1, Hastings had, nevertheless, become the first pilot to become a 'Diver' ace at the controls of a Merlin-engined Spitfire (text continues on page 43).

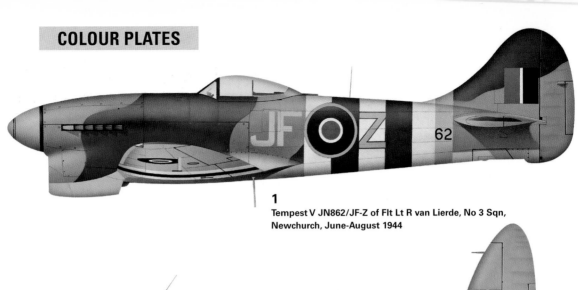

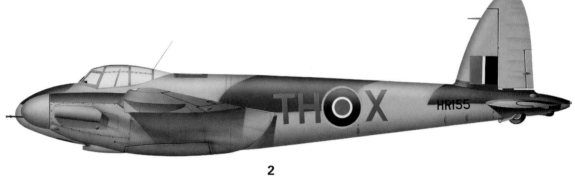

1
Tempest V JN862/JF-Z of Flt Lt R van Lierde, No 3 Sqn,
Newchurch, June-August 1944

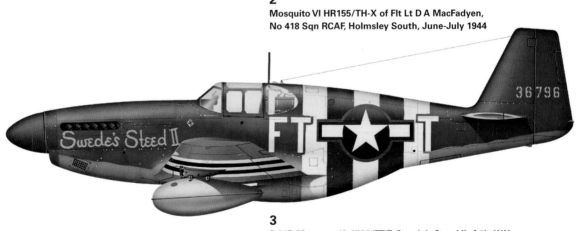

2
Mosquito VI HR155/TH-X of Flt Lt D A MacFadyen,
No 418 Sqn RCAF, Holmsley South, June-July 1944

3
P-51B Mustang 43-6796/FT-T *Swede's Steed II* of 1Lt W Y
Anderson, 353rd FS/354th FG, Lashenden, 17 June 1944

4
P-47D Thunderbolt 42-26919/E4-E *Shirley Jane III* of 1Lt E O
Fisher, 377th FS/362nd FG, Headcorn, 17 June 1944

5
Tempest V JN765/JF-K of Flg Off R H Clapperton,
No 3 Sqn, Newchurch, 18 June 1944

6
P-51D Mustang 44-13561/AJ-T of Maj R E Turner,
356th FS/354th FG, Lashenden, 18 June 1944

7
Tempest V JN769/JF-G of Flt Lt A R Moore,
No 3 Sqn, Newchurch, 19 June 1944

8
Spitfire XII MB856/EB-X of Flt Lt T Spencer, No 41 Sqn,
West Malling, 23 June 1944

9
Tempest V JN754/SA-A of Flt Lt H N Sweetman,
No 486 Sqn RNZAF, Newchurch, June-July 1944

10
Spitfire XIV NH714/RWO of Wg Cdr R W Oxspring, No 24 Wing,
Lympne, June-July 1944

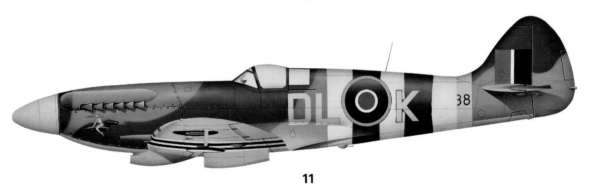

11
Spitfire XIV RB188/DL-K of Flt Lt H D Johnson, No 91 Sqn,
West Malling, June-July 1944

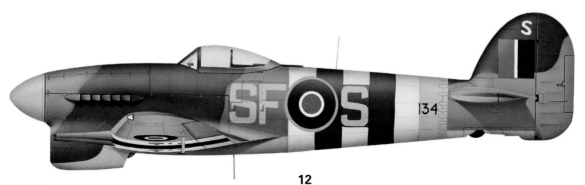

12
Typhoon IB MN134/SF-S of Flg Off A N Sames, No 137 Sqn,
Manston, June-July 1944

13
Tempest V JN801/SA-L of WO J H Stafford, No 486 Sqn RNZAF,
Newchurch, 30 June 1944

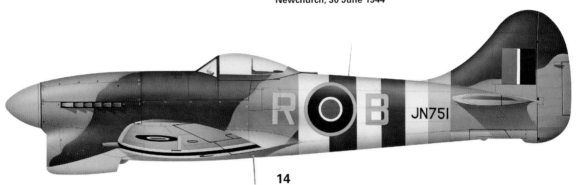

14
Tempest V JN751/RB of Wg Cdr R P Beamont, No 150 Wing,
Newchurch, July- August 1944

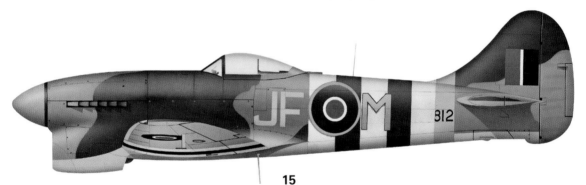

15
Tempest V JN812/JF-M of Sqn Ldr A S Dredge, No 3 Sqn
Newchurch, June-July 1944

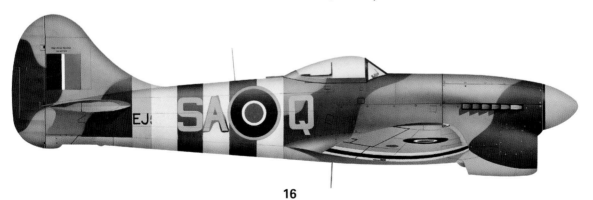

16
Tempest V EJ527/SA-Q of Flt Sgt O D Eagleson,
No 486 Sqn RNZAF, Newchurch, July 1944

17
Spitfire XIV RB159/DW-D of Sqn Ldr R A Newbery, No 610
'County of Chester' Sqn, Lympne, June-September 1944

18
Spitfire XIV NH654/DL-? of Capitaine J-M Maridor, No 91 Sqn,
West Malling, 7 July 1944

19
Spitfire XIV NH718/3W-G of Flg Off R F Burgwal,
No 322 (Dutch) Sqn, West Malling, 8 July 1944

20
Spitfire IX ML242/SK-A of Flt Lt J K Porteous, No 165 Sqn,
Lympne, 16 July 1944

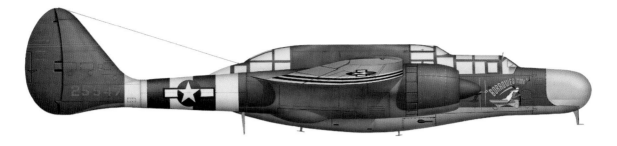

21
P-61A Black Widow 42-5547 *"BORROWED TIME"*
of 1Lt H E Ernst, 422nd NFS, Ford, 16 July 1944

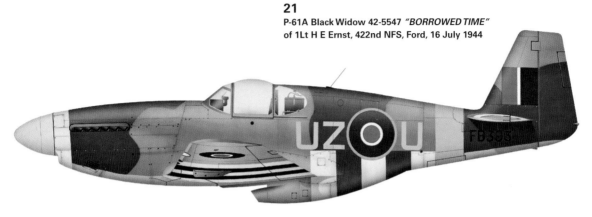

22
Mustang III FB393/UZ-U of Flt Sgt J Zalenski,
No 306 (Polish) Sqn, Brenzett, July-August 1944

23
Spitfire IX ML117/JX-D of Flg Off D H Davy, No 1 Sqn,
Lympne, July 1944

24
Mustang III FZ154/PK-N of Flt Lt M Cwynar,
No 315 (Polish) Sqn, Brenzett, 22 July 1944

25
Typhoon IB MN627/SF-N of Plt Off H T Nicholls,
No 137 Sqn, Manston, 31 July 1944

26
Meteor I EE222/YQ-G of Wg Cdr A McDowall,
No 616 'South Yorkshire' Sqn, Manston, August 1944

27
Mosquito XIX TA400/VY-J of Flg Off A J Owen No 85 Sqn,
West Malling, 4/5 August 1944

28
Mosquito XVII HK249/RX-B of Sqn Ldr G L Howitt,
No 456 Sqn RAAF, Ford, July-August 1944

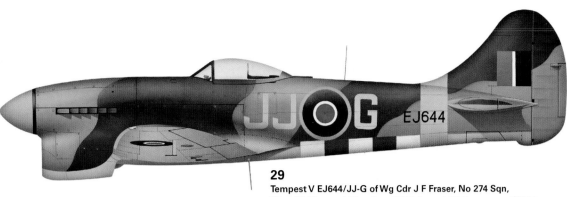

29
Tempest V EJ644/JJ-G of Wg Cdr J F Fraser, No 274 Sqn,
West Malling and Manston, 16/17 August 1944

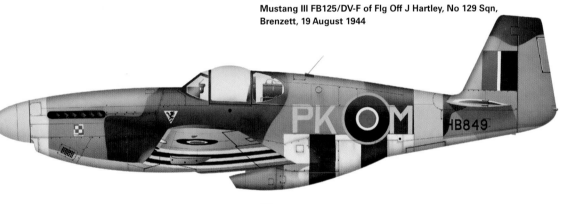

30
Mustang III FB125/DV-F of Flg Off J Hartley, No 129 Sqn,
Brenzett, 19 August 1944

31
Mustang III HB849/PK-M of Flt Lt J Schmidt, No 315 Sqn,
Brenzett, 20 August 1944

32
Tempest V EJ555/SD-Y of Flt Lt R L T Robb, No 501 'County of
Gloucester' Sqn, Bradwell Bay, 25/26 October 1944

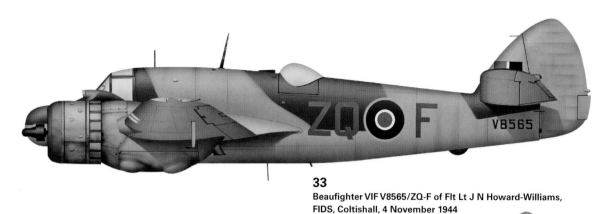

33
Beaufighter VIF V8565/ZQ-F of Flt Lt J N Howard-Williams,
FIDS, Coltishall, 4 November 1944

34
Mosquito XIII MM446/ZJ-Y of Wg Cdr E D Crew,
No 96 Sqn, Odiham, 15 November 1944

35
Tempest V EJ608/SD-P of Sqn Ldr A Parker-Rees, No 501
'County of Gloucester' Sqn, Bradwell Bay, 5 December 1944

36
Mustang III HB861/UZ-B of Flt Lt J Jeka, No 306 (Polish) Sqn,
Andrews Field, 6 March 1945

On 12 July Flg Off Hartley's squadronmate, and seven-victory ace, Flt Lt Desmond Ruchwaldy shot down the first of 8.5 V1s that he would eventually claim.

The number of pilots becoming V1 aces increased almost daily, with no fewer than seven reaching this status on 12 July alone. That day the fighter defences brought down 62 flying bombs, seven of them being credited to the Poles of No 316 Sqn. One of the pilots involved was WO Tadeusz Szymanski, who subsequently became one of the top V1 Mustang III aces with eight victories. During the afternoon of the 12th he shot a V1 down south of Dungeness, ensuring that he did not get too close to avoid the risk of debris damage. Almost immediately Szymanski was vectored onto another incoming 'Diver', and although he hit and slowed it down, his ammunition ran out.

'The thing was jerking along and the elevator was flapping with each vibration of the cruise jet motor', Szymanski later recalled. 'I noticed there were no ailerons, and also that on the front of the bomb was a silly little propeller. It looked ridiculous. I decided to try to tip the "Doodlebug" up with my wingtip. As soon as I put my port wing under the "Doodlebug's" wing it started lifting. I let it straighten itself out, then I put enough of the front part of my wingtip under its wingtip, taking care to keep my aileron out of the way, and then by a sharp bank to starboard I hit it with the port wingtip.' However, this failed to topple the bomb.

'I then tried a slightly different manoeuvre, hitting it very hard with my wingtip as I went up like in a loop. To my dismay the "Doodlebug" continued to fly on perfectly straight. Then I realised that the engine was now underneath. I had turned it upside down! I could see that it was gradually going into a dive, and then down it went.'

Szymanski repeated this feat again in early August. Two V1s also fell to his squadronmate Flt Sgt Alex Pietrzak on 12 July, and he would subsequently become a V1 ace in early August. Pietrzak was obliged to bail out of his Mustang III on the 12th, however, as his CO, Sqn Ldr Arct, recalled;

'In the heat of the fighting he closed in to 100 yards and opened accurate fire. He must have hit the fuses as the main bomb exploded in the air. The blast was so powerful that the Mustang lost its propeller and the wings bent to a most peculiar shape. The aircraft went out of control. Fortunately, Pietrzak, a stocky, well-built fellow, possessed very quick reflexes. His misfortune happened at 800 yards. He had lost quite a lot of precious height, and at the last moment he got out to save his life. Conclusions were drawn and we introduced the rule forbidding opening fire from less than 200 yards. This distance could easily be judged both in the daytime and at night.'

Pietrzak had been lucky to survive. Acts of bravery such as this had not gone unnoticed in Britain, and on 14 July Mosquito-equipped No 264 Sqn at Hartford Bridge, in Surrey, received some esteemed and unexpected visitors wishing to pass on their gratitude on behalf of the nation. Crews were lazily sauntering around the airfield in preparation for the night's activities, hands thrust into pockets and tunics undone, when a line of large, expensive cars appeared and out of the leading vehicle stepped the King and Queen! Surprised by the unscheduled Royal visit, the crews hastily made a semblance of a line in front of their Mosquitoes and, at the King's specific request, the aircrew were introduced in turn. They then took off on patrols, during which Flt Sgt Lee shot a V1 down off the French coast 'By Royal Command!'

Also up in a Tempest V that day was the FIU's CO, Wg Cdr Chris Hartley, who shot down a V1 to claim his only success. Sadly, his small unit lost another of its elite band of pilots on 16 July when the Tempest V flown by nine-victory ace Flt Lt Alan Wagner hit the ground in fog whilst chasing a missile. The same night Hartley, when chasing another V1, collided with a Mosquito of No 264 Sqn that was closing on the same target. Hartley managed to bail out, albeit with an injured ankle, but the Mosquito crew were killed.

BLACK WIDOWS

On 15/16 July a new type made its operational debut on anti-'Diver' missions. Having worked up at Scorton, in North Yorkshire, the USAAF's 422nd Night Fighter Squadron (NFS) sent a detachment of P-61A Black Widows to Ford for anti-V1 operations. 2Lt Herman Ernst and his radar operator Flt Off Ed Kopsel, flying their usual P-61A 42-5547 *"BORROWED TIME"* on the evening of 15 July, were vectored onto a V1. Using height to advantage, they down behind the target, only to have the excessive speed shatter the fighter's tail cone. Frustratingly, they had to return to base.

Airborne again the following night, they soon spotted four V1s, as Ernst recalled;

'It didn't take long to spot another "Diver". The scenario was similar to the previous night – dive down, line up behind it and open fire. This time we closed the gap and fired several 20 mm rounds. They found their mark all over the propulsion unit and the bomb lost power, nosed over and went into the sea. This was the 422nd's first kill of the war.'

On 15 July 2Lt Herman Ernst, flying from Ford with Flt Off Ed Kopsel in P-61A Black Widow 42-5547 *"BORROWED TIME"* of the 422nd NFS, claimed the type's first victory (*H Ernst via W Thompson*)

After moving onto mainland Europe, Herman Ernst went on to become one of a handful of P-61 aces. The 422nd's P-61s claimed further V1s on succeeding nights. One fell to Capt O Robert Elmore and his radar operator 2Lt Leonard Mapes flying P-61A 42-5534 *Shoo-Shoo-Baby* on 17 July, to which they later added four aircraft over the Continent. The next night it was the crew of *Tennessee Ridge Runner*, Lts John W Anderson and James W Mogan, who opened their combat account off the French coast, as Anderson vividly described;

'GCI picked up a "blip" that was in our area, and he gave us its speed and direction. At that time my radar operator pointed us in the right direction for an intercept. Minutes later, he was able to pick it up on his scope at a range of about eight miles – the chase was on! We closed in on the target from behind and above, Lt Mogan putting me in a perfect position to intercept. We had to get close enough to make a positive visual identification before firing. To reach a dead astern position it became necessary to dive down to attain a speed of about 400 mph in order to set up a satisfactory firing angle. I was in a perfect firing position, and let go with a burst that converged all over the V1's right wing. It was a perfect shot because it did not hit the warhead. The target rolled over and went straight into the ground. It was a perfect kill.'

However, two nights later, Capt Tadas Spelis and Flt Off Eleutherios Eleftherion, flying *Katy the Kid*, were lucky to survive their engagement, as Lt Guba, who had joined them as an observer, recalled;

'I was surprised to witness how close we were before we started firing. The first burst didn't seem to do anything but the second created a dangerous situation for us. One moment there was almost total darkness, and the next we were lit up like the sun had exploded. We had absolutely no time to move right or left, so we barrelled right through the centre of the fireball. It blinded everyone in the aircraft, and at the time we were diving at a low altitude. We could smell gasoline and feel the intense heat as we went through the explosion.'

Estimating target range at night was a constant problem during the anti-V1 campaign, as one pilot in the RAF's No 25 Sqn (flying Mosquito XVIIs), Flg Off Victor Linthune, explained;

'It was very difficult to work out the range with them. Some clever bloke came up with an optical contraption for distance calculations.'

He also recalled the ever-present problem of 'friendly fire';

'On the night of 22 July we got into position about 300 yards behind one, I opened fire and it blew up. Just at that moment the coastal "ack-ack" began, so there was a lot of debris flying around. There were certain areas where we weren't allowed to shoot at them and ground control would tell you to get out. You had to have luck on your side.'

Such luck had abandoned some of his contemporaries in No 96 Sqn on the night of 17/18 July. Sqn Ldr Alastair Parker-Rees and his navigator Flt Lt Geoffrey Bennett, having become a V1 ace team a few days earlier, were patrolling off the south coast when they had intercepted and shot down two more missiles. However, as they chased after a third they were fired on by an unknown assailant and forced to bail out into the Channel. After six hours in the sea they were rescued by the O-Class destroyer HMS *Obedient*.

A few days later the 422nd NFS, having destroyed four V1s, moved to France. During the unit's brief assignment to anti-V1 operations a number

No 3 Sqn CO Sqn Ldr Alan Dredge briefs his pilots at Newchurch around the tail of Tempest V JN812/JF-M. He shot down seven V1s in this aircraft, with other pilots destroying two more (*JT C Long*)

of RAF pilots had increased their haul. Among them was 22-year-old Flg Off Ray McPhie of No 91 Sqn, who had reached V1 acedom north of Beachy Head on the 18th when his target blew up;

'When you hit one and it exploded you really were tossed up. It was black, red – all the colours of the explosion – and you got a tremendous kick up the backside as you went up. It was quite a ride!'

The following day his Wing Leader, Wg Cdr Bobby Oxspring, destroyed his final 'Diver' to give him V1 ace status. As a result of this success he had joined a select group of aviators who had 'made ace' against both manned and unmanned aircraft.

A few hours earlier, during the night of 18/19 July, Flt Lts Branse Burbridge and Bill Skelton of No 85 Sqn had chased two V1s in their Mosquito and been credited with destroying one of them. Burbridge, who subsequently became the leading Allied nightfighter pilot of World War 2, wrote in his log book the enigmatic entry, 'Why?' Most of the time he entered, 'No Joy (again!)'. He too recalled the problem of night vision. 'One difficulty was loss of night vision following the explosion of a missile, so to compensate we resorted to closing one eye before opening fire'.

Although in France the Allied armies had made steady advances in Normandy since D-Day, these had, as yet, had little effect on the intensity of the V1 bombardment. However, the threat posed by the overrunning of the launch sites was recognised by the Germains, although it was Allied air power that still provided the major counter to the offensive, with 'Noball' sites being regularly attacked. Yet it was probably the interdiction and disruption of the logistics and supply chains that gave the enemy the greatest headache. For now, it was the fighters, guns and barrage balloons that provided the key defence for the cities of southern England as they continued to be targeted by V1s.

Flg Off Dennis Davy of No 1 Sqn was one of just a handful of pilots to become a V1 ace flying the Merlin-engined Spitfire IX (*Goss/Rauchbach Archive*)

The Mustang III units now hit their stride, and on 22 July four squadrons flying the American fighter brought down 34 V1s between them. The Tempest V squadrons also had a successful day, bringing down 28 – including three more to Wg Cdr 'Bea' Beamont. The most successful of his units was No 3 Sqn, whose pilots claimed 16. Two of these fell to the CO, Sqn Ldr Alan Dredge, who had taken his score to 4.5 some days earlier and now claimed his final flying bombs.

On 23 July the honours again went to No 3 Sqn, with 11 of its pilots bringing down 13 more missiles. Flying a Spitfire XII from Lympne, in Kent, Flg Off Maurice Balasse of No 41 Sqn shared in the destruction of his fifth V1 to become an ace – a feat he shared that day with Flg Off Dennis Davy of No 1 Sqn. The third pilot to down his fifth V1 on the 23rd was Flg Off Peter Brooke, who became No 264 Sqn's sole 'Diver' ace when he shot down two flying bombs to add to the trio that he had claimed three nights earlier.

The night of 23/24 July saw a record set for the number of V1s destroyed in a single sortie and, almost inevitably, the pilot was the FIU's irrepressible Flt Lt Joe Berry. One of his contemporaries in the unit was Flt Lt Jeremy Howard-Williams, who recounted how Berry had shot down seven in a single night, the last of which had exploded. 'A fragment of bomb must have hit part of his aircraft for he felt the shock. The Tempest veered sharply'. One of the Tempest V's fuel tanks now read empty, having been holed, and the radio had ceased to function. 'Carefully descending through cloud over the sea, he flew until he recognised the coastline', Howard-Williams concluded. Of his record making and gutsy sortie, Berry modestly recorded in his log book, '7 destroyed. Petrol tank exploded. R/T u/s'.

Multiple claims were no stranger to Berry, however, for a few days earlier he had brought down five, including one during daylight hours in the most appalling weather. On the 25th he shot down four more, then on the night of 27 July he pursued one at low-level over West Malling airfield, closing to within 100 ft in order to ensure that he destroyed it before it fell on the base. Berry's own aircraft was damaged in the resulting explosion, but to his obvious chagrin, on this occasion he had to share this success with the crew of a Mosquito who had opened fire from 1000 yards and that, in the opinion of the FIU, had missed!

Following the recent losses to the FIU Tempest Flight, these successes proved a great boost to morale. By then the FIU total had reached 50, of

which Berry had claimed 36.5, making him the leading V1 ace by some margin – a position he was to retain. He was not the only pilot to have a narrow squeak at this time, as No 41 Sqn's diary for the 29 July described;

'A flying bomb was intercepted head-on flying at 3000 ft off Le Touquet. Flg Off M A L Balasse, diving from 7000 ft, misjudged his approach and narrowly missed a collision as he passed under the bomb. Pulling up to come back to the attack, he saw the bomb crash into the sea.'

REVOLUTIONARY EQUIPMENT

By this time the strategy for the defences had changed, with the Spitfire XIVs of Nos 91 and 322 Sqns having been moved forward to Deanland advanced landing ground in Kent to be better able to catch the 'Divers' approaching the coast. The day fighter defences also received a significant and groundbreaking reinforcement in the shape of the RAF's first Meteor jets. No 616 'South Yorkshire' Sqn had begun re-equipment earlier in July, and under its new CO, Battle of Britain ace Wg Cdr Andrew McDowall, its Meteor Flight had swiftly worked up.

On 27 July No 616 Sqn Meteor Is flown by Flg Offs Dean and McKenzie and Sqn Ldr Watts completed the unit's first 'Diver' patrols. Les Watts, who was a successful pilot from the fighting over Malta and had been CO until the arrival of McDowall and the jets, spotted a flying bomb and easily caught up with it over Ashford, but his cannon jammed when he tried to shoot the V1 down. To the squadron's intense frustration problems with the four Hispano Mk III cannon would plague early operations with the Meteor I. Nevertheless, the unit's diarist proudly wrote;

'Today the Meteors go onto operations. History is made! At 1430 hrs Flg Off McKenzie [flying EE219/YQ-D] took off for a patrol line between Ashford and Robertsbridge. This mission was followed with other uneventful patrols by Wg Cdr McDowall [EE222/YQ-G], Wg Cdr Wilson [EE221/HJW], Flg Off Rodger [EE217/YQ-B] and WO

Flying Spitfire IX ML117/JX-D, Flg Off Dennis Davy of No 1 Sqn shot down 2.5 flying bombs, including his last two on 26 July (*Wg Cdr D G Cox*)

The only Typhoon pilot to become a V1 ace was Flg Off 'Artie' Sames of No 137 Sqn, who is the central figure in this photograph. He also had 2.5 claims against aircraft (*via C H Thomas*)

Wilkes [EE213/YQ-A]. Sqn Ldr Watts suffered gun trouble when lined up on a V1, while Flg Off Dean [EE218/YQ-C] chased one as far as the balloon barrage. Between 1825 hrs and 1910 hrs, the CO flew another patrol [in EE219/YQ-D].'

The revolutionary Meteor I was not the only new weapon the RAF deployed against the flying bombs. Following the unleashing of a salvo of 60-lb rockets against a V1 the previous month, quantities of trial rockets with proximity fuses were delivered to No 137 Sqn for carriage on its Typhoons. Flg Off 'Artie' Sames became the first to use the new weapon when he attacked a V1 on 27 July, but on his first attack the rockets exploded about 40 ft above the flying bomb, which, to his chagrin, continued on its way! Sames had, however, already brought down four V1s by more conventional cannon fire during the previous month's engagements.

The following night Flg Off Doug Brandreth, flying a Typhoon equipped with the special rockets, intercepted a V1 over the sea as it approached Folkestone at 320 mph at a height of 3000 ft. Closing in to about 500 yards astern, he released a pair of rockets and these too exploded above the missile. Moments later the V1's engine flamed out and it crashed into the sea, thus making Brandreth the only pilot to down a 'Diver' with this imaginative weapon.

That same night (28/29 July) Flt Lt Bob Cowper, a six-victory ace flying Mosquitoes with No 456 Sqn, claimed his solitary V1 success. He reported that 'many strikes were seen but visual lost shortly afterwards. However, the Royal Observer Corps confirmed that a flying bomb exploded on the ground at 2356 hrs'. Interestingly, Cowper also reported that he had seen a long wire trailing from the missile.

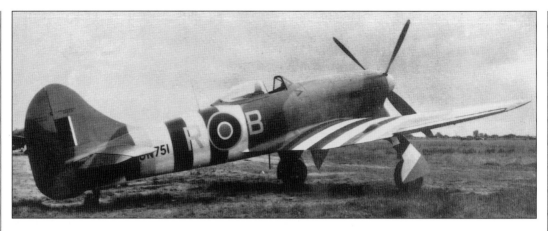

Tempest V JN751/RB was the personal mount of the leader of No 150 Wg, Wg Cdr 'Bea' Beamont, who claimed 16 and two shared V1s destroyed in it from his total of 26 and five shared. He was the fourth most successful pilot against flying bombs. Beamont later led his wing onto the Continent and claimed the last of his 6.5 victories against aircraft in JN751 (*R P Beamont via C H Thomas*)

At about the same time squadronmate Flg Off Fred Stevens was also in action, shooting down two to claim his only successes. These kills took the squadron's total to ten, although he noted that the Mosquito XVIIs were too slow and he looked forward to receiving faster Mk XXXs.

Another Mosquito pilot, Flt Lt Keith Panter of No 25 Sqn, shot down two V1s that night, describing the end of the second flying bomb as follows;

'I dived to slightly below the target and opened fire from 800 ft dead astern. Strikes were observed on the propulsion unit, and the flying bomb emitted large quantities of sparks. I broke away to port, intending to position myself for a further attack, but I saw the flying bomb dive vertically down and explode on land.'

Panter was to finish with a total of four V1s destroyed and a probable. Also up on 28/29 July was Wg Cdr 'Bea' Beamont in his personally marked Tempest V, who shot down his 27th flying bomb. During daylight hours on 28 July five more pilots had become V1 aces, whilst the following evening No 315 Sqn's charismatic leader Sqn Ldr Eugeniusz 'Dziubek' Horbaczewski shot down two to also become a V1 ace.

The night of 29/30 July brought No 96 Sqn CO Wg Cdr Edward Crew his penultimate engagement with a V1. Also in action from his squadron was Flt Lt 'Togs' Mellersh, who shot down his 22nd flying bomb.

To assist the nightfighters in their quest to destroy flying bombs, the FIU had carried out the first trials of the Monica III E tail warning radar as a range indicator from its home base at Wittering, in Cambridgeshire, earlier that month. The equipment was installed in a borrowed Mosquito VI, and instead of pointing backwards, it was fitted in reverse so as to become a forward-looking system. The results were encouraging, and the Telecommunications Research Establishment at Defford, in Worcestershire, fitted Tempest V EJ535 with Monica III E equipment for operational trials by the FIU – it was delivered to Newchurch on 30 July.

The perils of V1 operations were once again highlighted on 31 July when No 91 Sqn suffered a severe blow. Flying Spitfire XIV RM654, Flg Off Paddy Schade was chasing a V1 in poor visibility when he collided with No 486's Sqn Flt Sgt Archie Wilson in a Tempest V as he too closed on the same target. Both men died. It was a sad end for Schade, who had survived the maelstrom of the fighting in Malta with 12 victories to his name.

THE BATTLE IS WON

August began quietly, but this changed at 1302 hrs on the 2nd when a flying bomb struck a restaurant in Beckenham, killing 44 and injuring many more. It was during this lunchtime barrage that No 3 Sqn's Flt Sgt Bert Bailey, an Australian, shot down his final V1s to take his total to 14. At the same time No 91 Sqn's Flt Lt Ray Nash also attacked a brace to make his last claims, increasing his total to 20. During the second engagement the 'Diver' was also attacked by Flt Sgt Ronnie van Beers of No 322 Sqn, giving the Dutch unit its 100th success when Nash sportingly withdrew his claim. It also elevated the Dutch NCO to V1 ace status. His Combat Report stated, 'Attacked with three short bursts, 350 yards line astern. "Diver" went into shallow dive through cloud and believed to have crashed near balloon barrage in Tunbridge Wells'. Within minutes Nash's CO, and fellow V1 ace, Sqn Ldr Peter Bond also made his final claim when he blew up another missile.

As July had ended a further Tempest V unit was preparing for action, No 501 Sqn swapping its Spitfire IXs for the Hawker fighter. Among the unit's pilots was Sgt 'Ben' Gunn, who after the war became an accomplished test pilot. He recalled the first Tempest V being delivered to the squadron at Westhampnett, in West Sussex, by a slight female ATA pilot. 'The CO looked at me and said, "If she can fly it, so can you – get airborne!"' Gunn noted in his log book after his first flight, 'This is a real aeroplane – AND HOW!'

On 2 August No 501 Sqn moved forward to Manston in preparation to join the V1 defences. The following day the FIU Tempest Flight began trials with Monica-equipped aircraft when Flt Lt Cyril Thornton conducted a test flight. The modified fighter was also flown during daylight hours by the FIU's USAAF pilot, Flt Off 'Bud' Miller.

Although ADGB units achieved some notable successes on 2 August, it also proved to be a day of tragedy for the defenders, as Wg Cdr Bobby Oxspring described in his autobiography;

'In a chase over Kent, French pilot Capitaine Jean Maridor of No 91 Sqn fired and hit a target in the tail control, causing it to dive. To his consternation he saw it falling directly on a military field hospital, identified by a large red cross in the grounds. Many witnesses testified that the gallant Frenchman, not having time to set up another firing attack, deliberately rammed the warhead, which exploded and killed him.

'Shortly afterwards, Flt Lt "Gin" Seagers, a Belgian attached to the same squadron, lost his life within sight of the airfield when he attacked a target from an awkward angle of fully 90 degrees. Trying to pull enough deflection, he lost sight of it under his nose and misjudged the distance. To our horror he struck the warhead, which in a deadly second demolished both target and Spitfire.'

The loss of these two pilots, and of Paddy Schade three days earlier, was a sad end to No 91's V1 campaign, as the unit was withdrawn from the role a few days later. By then it was the leading Spitfire unit, having

51

brought down more than 180 V1s. Re-equipped with Spitfire IXs and tasked with flying bomber escort duties from 14 August, the squadron lost its CO the following day during one of its first missions. Sqn Ldr Norman Kynaston, who had shot down 22 V1s, was hit by flak and lost. He was replaced by another V1 ace, Sqn Ldr Peter Bond.

Throughout the morning of 3 August ADGB units flying a variety of fighter types had been active. No 129 Sqn's Mustang III pilots shot down seven and shared in the destruction of an eighth, with Flt Lt 'Dutch' Kleimeyer of the RAAF achieving ace status. That night Flt Lt Peter Leggat of No 418 Sqn, flying a Mosquito VI with navigator Flt Lt Frank Cochrane, described the tactics used when shooting down his fourth V1 that they had spotted heading northwest at 2000 ft over the Channel north of Le Touquet;

'Our aircraft was then flying across the sea from Dieppe to Le Touquet at 9000 ft, and we turned to port on the track of the "Diver", diving down in an attempt to overshoot but pulling up astern when reaching the same altitude. At 400 yards range, three short bursts of cannon and machine gun were given and our aircraft broke off as the "Diver" was pulling away at indicated air speed 400. Immediately afterwards the light on the flying bomb was seen to go out. The "Diver" hit the sea and exploded on impact.'

Leggat shot down his fifth to achieve acedom on 6/7 August.

The honours for 3/4 August probably belonged to No 96 Sqn, however, as the unit diarist excitedly described. 'What a night! Nine "Divers" knocked down by two crews!' During an incredible sortie between 0115 hrs and 0322 hrs Flt Lt 'Togs' Mellersh shot down seven V1s off Dungeness to equal Joe Berry's record sortie. His CO, Wg Cdr Edward Crew, downed another two off Dover to take his total to 21 – these were his final victories over flying bombs. Interestingly, in a hint at a possible change of enemy tactics, Crew also reported that they appeared to be coming as a regular stream, rather than the salvos that had previously been noted. Two hours earlier Flt Lt Doug Brandreth of No 137 Sqn had been up in his Typhoon fitted with the special proximity fused rockets, but having made two unsuccessful attacks using them he eventually resorted to his cannon to bring down his fourth, and final, V1.

Although No 96 Sqn's two crews had bagged nine, the FIU's small Tempest Flight went two better, claiming eleven – five were credited to Joe Berry. That same night Flt Lt Cyril Thornton began his path to becoming a 'Diver' ace when he shot down two, whilst the first of the two that Flt Lt 'Jackson' Robb destroyed made him a V1 ace.

One of August's casualties was Capitaine Jean-Marie Maridor of No 91 Sqn, who died in heroic circumstances on the 3rd (*R M Batten*)

The revolutionary Meteor I jet fighters of No 616 Sqn had their combat debut against the V1 in the summer of 1944. EE222/YQ-G was the personal aircraft of the CO, Battle of Britain ace Wg Cdr Andrew McDowall, and it wore his rank pennant on the port side of the nose. He crash-landed in it near Manston on 29 August (*T R Allonby*)

The distinction of claiming the RAF's first jet victory went to Flg Off 'Dixie' Dean when on 4 August he brought down a V1 by 'tipping' after his fighter had suffered cannon failure (*G R Pitchfork*)

AN HISTORIC FIRST

By this time the Meteor Is of No 616 Sqn had been conducting anti-V1 patrols from Manston for a week, but despite several close calls, success had so far eluded them. Haze and poor visibility prevented any flying during the morning of 4 August, but it had improved sufficiently by mid-afternoon to allow Flg Offs 'Dixie' Dean and 'Jock' Rodger to scramble on a patrol over central Kent in good visibility on a sunny afternoon on what was to prove a historic sortie. Dean described how he established his unique niche in RAF history;

'At 1545 hrs I was scrambled under "Kinsley 11" Control for an anti-"Diver" patrol between Ashford and Robertsbridge. Flying at 4500 ft and 340 mph, I saw one "Diver" four to five miles southeast of Tenterden flying at 1000 ft on a course of 330 degrees at an estimated speed of 365 mph, at 1616 hrs. From 2.5 miles behind the "Diver" I dived down from 4500 ft at 470 mph. Closing in to attack, I found my four 20 mm guns would not fire owing to technical trouble now being investigated. I then flew my Meteor alongside the "Diver" for approximately 20-30 seconds. Gradually, I manoeuvred my wingtip a few inches under the wing of the "Diver", then pulling my aircraft sharply upwards I turned it over on to its back and sent it diving to earth approximately four miles south of Tonbridge. On return to Manston I was informed that the Royal Observer Corps had confirmed one "Diver" had crashed at the position given by me. This is the first pilotless aircraft to be destroyed by a jet-propelled aircraft.'

Shortly afterwards Flg Off 'Jock' Rodger found another V1 that he attacked in a more conventional way using his battery of 20 mm cannon;

'At 1640 hrs I sighted a "Diver" over Tenterden flying on a course of 318 degrees at 3000 ft and a speed of 340 mph. I immediately attacked from astern and fired a two-second burst at a range of 300 yards. I observed hits and petrol and/ or oil streaming out of the "Diver", which continued to fly

53

straight and level. I fired another two-second burst from my four cannon still from 300 yards. Both myself and the "Diver" were flying at 340 mph. The Diver then went down, and I saw it explode on the ground about five miles northwest of Tonbridge.'

No 616 Sqn's diarist penned in the daily report, 'The Squadron, now thrilled at the first two kills, is ready for more'.

Earlier that same day No 137 Sqn's Flg Off 'Artie' Sames had also gained himself a small, but unique, niche in the annals of the RAF when, in bringing down his fifth and final 'Diver', he became the only pilot to achieve V1 ace status whilst flying the mighty Typhoon. The afternoon of the 4th had seen Tempest V pilots from No 56 Sqn in the thick of the action too, including Plt Off David Ness who downed two flying bombs over Kent to make him a V1 ace – he subsequently claimed 5.5 aircraft shot down as well. Also 'making ace' that day was New Zealander Plt Off Keith Smith of No 486 Sqn, who brought down three V1s between the Kentish towns of Tunbridge Wells and Maidstone.

About 30 minutes after Smith's success, 37-year-old Grp Capt Tadeusz Nowierski, CO of No 133 (Polish) Wing, proved that V1 hunting was not just a young

man's game when, flying his personally marked Mustang III, he shot a 'Diver' down near New Romney, in Kent. His fellow exiles in No 322 Sqn were also active at the same time, with Flt Lt Jan van Arkel shooting down his final V1 and Flt Lt Jan Plesman claiming his tenth, reporting, 'I saw a "Diver" heading in over Eastbourne. Intercepted and attacked in dive, firing from 200 yards. "Diver" exploded on ground two miles north of Hailsham'.

Early the following morning (5 August), No 418 Sqn's successful team of Sqn Ldr Russ Bannock and Flg Off Bob Bruce had their penultimate V1 engagement when, over the Channel, they shot down two and

Commander of the Polish-manned No 133 Wing was 37-year-old Grp Capt Tadeusz Nowierski, who proved that V1 hunting was not just a young man's game! (*via W Matusiak*)

When Nowierski shot down his only V1, on 5 August, he was flying his personally marked, and immaculate, Mustang III HB886/TN (*PI and SM via Wojtek Matusiak*)

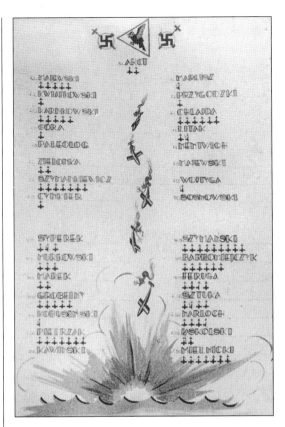

The Poles of No 316 Sqn kept a tote of their V1 victories using this detailed scoreboard. The stylised Swastikas seen on either side of the unit emblem were painted under the cockpits of successful aircraft to denote individual victories (*PI and SM via Wojtek Matusiak*)

damaged a third to take their total to 19. Over Sussex ten minutes later, just as dawn was breaking, No 456 Sqn's Flt Lt Keith Roediger shot down his fourth, the unit diarist by now using sporting metaphors in his reports. 'Last night Flt Lt Roediger/Flt Lt Dobson downed another in the "Diver handicap" which exploded on the ground at approximately 0500 hrs'. Two nights later (6/7 August) Keith Roediger and his navigator Flt Lt R J H Dobson became No 456 Sqn's first V1 ace crew when they destroyed their fifth – their target was flying over land at low-level.

Dawn had barely broken on 5 August when No 316 Sqn's Mustang IIIs were in action as the stream of V1s heading towards southern England from their launch sites in the Pas de Calais continued. Among the pilots who made claims was Flt Sgt Alex Pietrzak, the first of the two he brought down making him a V1 ace. Later in the day two of No 322 Sqn's aces, Flg Offs Jan Jonker and Rudi Burgwal, both increased their scores, the former making his final claim. Their colleagues in No 610 Sqn, with whom there was a friendly rivalry, also continued to contribute when Australian Flt Lt Tony Gaze (an experienced ace with eight victories) destroyed a V1. Although the missile had approached him from behind, he was able to turn quickly, close on the 'Diver' and open fire. In spite of many patrols, however, this proved to be Gaze's only success against a flying bomb. Success for some, however, came in multiples, with the FIU's Flt Lt Berry – flying several rare daytime patrols – shooting down five during the course of the day!

One of No 316 Sqn's nine V1 aces was Flt Sgt Aleksander Pietrzak, who also eventually claimed 3.5 aircraft destroyed too (*PI and SM via Wojtek Matusiak*)

Flying over Robertsbridge on 5 August, No 165 Sqn's Flg Off 'Ac' Lawson claimed his fifth V1 to become the latest Spitfire IX 'Diver' ace. In what proved to be a lively encounter with the missile, the '"Diver" blew up immediately following a half-second burst, causing minor damage to my Spitfire and throwing it on its side'. Ten minutes later, over Tunbridge Wells, he spotted another V1 that was being fired on by a Tempest V but without effect, as he noted in his Combat Report. 'Tempest pulled out to one side and I attacked. Second burst caused "Diver" to explode. Spitfire again clobbered by explosion, causing damage to hood'.

Lawson's squadronmate Plt Off Lewin brought down No 165 Sqn's last flying bomb just 90 minutes later, taking the unit's total to 60 (one of them shared). This tally made it the most successful Merlin-engined Spitfire squadron of the campaign by some measure.

Perhaps the day's most significant event was the arrival on the scene of No 501 Sqn. Having rapidly re-equipped with the Tempest V, the unit was transferred from Westhampnett to Manston on 2 August. Three days later Flg Off Bill Polley claimed No 501 Sqn's first missile with the Tempest V;

'I shot down six V1s and shared one, and, like other pilots, I shot at others but had no confirmation of success. The area of chase was very limited, as we patrolled between the coastal batteries that fired at everything that moved – including us – and the barrage balloons. We had minutes at most to find our target, get into position and fire. Very often we were too close to our targets before we got the opportunity to fire, and the big danger was getting an airburst. On one occasion I was chasing a V1 too quickly, and I knew that I was overhauling the bomb too rapidly. I fired a long burst and pulled up steeply to starboard, placing me almost directly above the V1 just as it exploded. The blast caught my left wing and sent the aircraft tumbling in a series of snap rolls. After what seemed an eternity the Tempest regained its stability. As my gyros had tumbled, it took me a while to realise that I was upside down.'

No 501 Sqn was not the only unit to engage V1s for the first time on 5 August, for as darkness fell the second USAAF Black Widow squadron (425th NFS) to be declared operational claimed its first 'Diver' when Lts Garth Peterson and John Howe bagged one. The following night they shot down another to become the only P-61 crew to make multiple V1 claims. Two more missiles were destroyed before the 425th NFS moved to the Continent later in the month.

Also airborne on the night of 5/6 August were Mustang IIIs of No 316 Sqn. Shortly after midnight over the sea off Newhaven, in East Sussex, Flt Lt Teofal Szymankiewicz blew one up – the first of nine for the Polish unit on what was to be its best day of the campaign. Szymankiewicz would become a V1 ace within a few days. No 316 Sqn was to bring down eight more on the 7th, and a 'Diver' also fell to the leading Dutch V1 ace, Flg Off Rudi Burgwal, on this date – his 24th, and last, success against a flying bomb. Burgwal noted in his Combat Report;

'When coming in to land I was told by flying control that a "Diver" was over base. Gave chase and attacked line astern, range 150 yards. The light went out and "Diver" went into a glide. Noted red light warning was near balloon barrage. As turned for base saw glare from explosion and felt blast.'

In early August No 501 Sqn was re-equipped with Tempest Vs and absorbed the Tempest Flight of the FIU. Amongst the pilots to transfer from the latter was Rhodesian night intruder ace Flg Off Leo Williams (*author's collection*)

Three days later the Dutchmen flew their final 'Diver' patrol before handing over their Spitfire XIVs. No 322 Sqn's final total was 108 V1s destroyed, with Burgwal being the unit's top scorer.

No 616 Sqn's Meteor Is also continued to make a modest contribution, six jets being scrambled at dawn on 7 August. 'Dixie' Dean was again successful a short while later, as was recorded by the unit's Intelligence Officer;

'At approximately 0620 hrs Flg Off Dean, who was flying at a height of 1000 ft, intercepted a "Diver" approximately four miles east of Robertsbridge. The "Diver" was flying at 1000 ft on a course of 330 degrees at a speed estimated at 390 mph. Flg Off Dean came in to attack from line astern at 400 mph and opened fire with all four cannon at 700 yards. The pilot continued firing in short bursts, closing in to 500 yards. Strikes were seen and pieces fell off the "Diver's" starboard wing. Finally Dean broke away, having expended his ammunition, and saw the "Diver" go down in a shallow dive. It was not possible to see the "Diver" crash owing to prevailing ground mist. It was later confirmed by the Royal Observer Corps that the "Diver" had crashed at 0625 hrs.'

The teething troubles with the Meteor I's guns remained, however, as Flg Off Mike Cooper explained;

'The problem with the guns was caused by an updraught in the underfuselage ejector slots, preventing the empty shell cases from being ejected. Once modifications had been made the guns fired perfectly.'

Once darkness fell on 7 August, the FIU's Tempest Vs were active once again, shooting down eight – Flt Lt Berry almost inevitably claimed the majority of the victims, although significantly one also fell to Flg Off Leo Williams. The Rhodesian was an established Mosquito night intruder ace who thus began his path to also becoming a V1 ace. Berry's claims took him past his 'half-century' and resulted in him being awarded a bar to his DFC. Also making multiple claims through the night of 7/8 August was 'Togs' Mellersh, of No 96 Sqn, who brought down four. Two were whilst flying his usual Mosquito, but the first two were shot down flying Spitfire IX MH473, which he had borrowed from the Night Fighting Development Wing!

Another nightfighter ace to enjoy success that evening was No 157 Sqn's Flt Lt 'Jimmy' Matthews, who used his Mosquito XIX to down two missiles. 'First dived and exploded on the ground. Second exploded in the air, damaging my aircraft'. Matthews became a V1 ace with these victories.

Despite the prodigious efforts of the fighters and the AA, flying bombs kept falling on London, where the casualties continued to mount.

On 10 August No 501 Sqn underwent a significant and complicated change. Sqn Ldr Gary Barnett and many of his pilots moved across to No 274 Sqn, which was replacing its Spitfire IXs with Tempest Vs in the day fighter role at Manston. Joe Berry was promoted to squadron leader and given command of No 501 Sqn, his FIU Tempest Flight being absorbed into what was effectively a new squadron. Flt Lts 'Jackson' Robb and Cyril Thornton, Flg Offs 'Lucky' Lucas and Leo Williams and American Flt Off 'Bud' Miller, all of whom were, or would become, V1 aces, provided an able and experienced core to the new No 501 Sqn. The unit also retained some of its original cadre of pilots, including night flying veteran and future V1 ace Flg Off Bill Polley. Additional pilots were posted in, among them ex-No 68 Sqn Mosquito pilot Flg Off Gilbert Wild;

'We were greeted by the Commanding Officer, Sqn Ldr Joe Berry DFC and two Bars, and our Flight Commander "Jackson" Robb, another ace. The boys in the crewroom made us very welcome, and they were very bright and cheerful, despite the number of recent losses. "Jackson" had given me a copy of the Pilot's Notes, and after I had completed a quick perusal of them, he took me out to a Tempest and sat me in the cockpit. Having given me a quick check of the cockpit drill, he told me "Off you go, three circuits and bumps. Hard left rudder on takeoff and landing, otherwise you'll swing like a bitch! And don't bend it – we're short!"

'The Tempest V also had some new fuel – 150 octane petrol, yes 150 octane. It was, in fact, 100 octane with extra tetra-ethyl-lead to give added boost. This allowed us to takeoff at +24 boost, and use this setting for high speed when necessary. The snag was that the engine had to be cleared at full throttle and maximum revs about every 15 minutes, otherwise the plugs would soon get fouled up. Doing this at night for the first time gave one quite a shock – sparks would cascade from the exhausts, giving the impression of being on fire!'

Having formed his single-seater unit specifically for night anti-V1 duties, Berry was summoned to London, where he was bluntly told what was expected of No 501 Sqn. What he then briefed to his pilots upon his return was chilling, and showed the ruthless approach to total war from Britain's political leadership;

'I was called away yesterday and received instructions about the role of 501 against the night intruder. It was said to me that these instructions came from the Prime Minister himself, to the effect that the squadron must consider itself expendable, and thus will take off to try to effect interception in every weather condition, even though all other squadrons are grounded. This measure is being taken because it is felt that the threat of the V1 is so great that the people on the ground must at least "hear" fighters airborne whenever there is a V1 warning. The squadron will, therefore, get airborne even if it is quite impossible to make any interception.'

As the leading anti-V1 pilot, Berry had also been instructed to attend a press facility, where he said;

'Our chief difficulty was that although we could see the bombs much further away at night, we could not easily judge how far away they were. All we could do at first was to fly alongside the fairly slow bombs and remember what they looked like at lethal range. In this way a very good interception system was worked out before the new range finder was issued.'

The stark reality of these instructions to No 501 Sqn was explained by Plt Off Ron Bennett;

'The patrols were quite long – two hours or more – flying between searchlights that marked the patrol boundaries. Our expendability was brought home to us on many occasions when we were sent off in all sorts

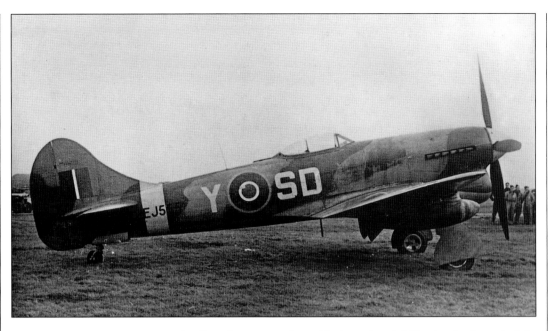

Leo Williams' third V1, but first with No 501 Sqn, was destroyed when flying Tempest V EJ555/SD-Y. V1 aces Flt Lt Cyril Thonton and 'Jackson' Robb also made claims when flying this machine (*via C H Thomas*)

of weather – very often with the real probability that by the end of the patrol the airfield would be covered in fog or low cloud. In fact, on one occasion, I went off when the Met forecaster had predicted that the only airfield open at the end of the period would be Valley, in Anglesey. Luckily the timing was wrong and I managed to get back into Manston before the fog rolled in.'

Whilst the bulk of the V1 successes fell to those units allocated to the task, others also made contributions, including Mosquito XVII-equipped No 125 Sqn. One of the unit's flight commanders was Sqn Ldr Eric Barwell, a distinguished nightfighter ace. He described how, on the night of 10 August, he brought down one of the six V1s credited to his squadron during the anti-'Diver' campaign;

'I made several interceptions but only managed to hit one or two. The difficulty was that the V1 was faster than the Mosquito flying straight and level. I realised that I must gain considerable height advantage and attack with the greater speed achieved in a dive. On one occasion I saw the flames of the ram jet, dived and fired, closing in to around 100 ft. Suddenly the bomb exploded and I was completely blinded. When my night vision returned I struggled to control the aircraft as it was buffeted by the explosion. We later found a couple of pieces of shrapnel in the Mosquito.'

The 'new' No 501 Sqn was, of course immediately operational, and on 11/12 August (the night after its reformation) the unit shot down eight V1s. Three of these were claimed by Flt Lt Cyril Thornton just before midnight, giving him ace status. As Thornton returned to Manston, 'Bud' Miller departed, as the American recalled in his Combat Report;

'The first "Diver" was seen at 0017 hrs coming from the southwest at 1000 ft and 350 mph on a course of 235 degrees. I fired three two-second bursts from 50 yards and saw pieces fall off. The "Diver" went down and crashed eight miles east of Tonbridge. The second "Diver" was spotted at 0125 hrs with the same height and speed as the first. I fired from 100 yards astern. The "Diver" crashed and exploded a few miles northeast of Tonbridge.'

With its destruction Miller became the sole USAAF V1 ace, albeit whilst serving with the RAF. He then continued his patrol;

'The third "Diver" was seen north of Sandwich at 8000 ft on a course of 290 degrees at 280 mph. I attacked and fired four two-second bursts from 500 yards astern. I saw the "Diver" explode on the ground at 0135 hrs, approximately 30 seconds after my last burst.'

Miller's CO, Joe Berry, continued to harvest his regular crop of flying bombs too when, on the 12th, he shot down a V1, despatching two more in daylight the next day. Another one fell to his guns on the night of 14 August, and two more on the night of the 16th. Berry's marksmanship had by now become nothing less than remarkable. Indeed, he had become so accurate that on one occasion he destroyed a missile following the expenditure of just 60 rounds.

THE CRISIS PASSES

As well as the personnel swap in No 501 Sqn, there had been other significant changes to the order of battle over the preceding few days. On 9 August Nos 91 and 322 Sqns handed their Spitfires XIVs over to Nos 350 (Belgian) and 402 Sqns at Hawkinge, while No 130 Sqn had moved to Lympne after it too had converted to Mk XIVs. No 165 Sqn had also ceased 'Diver' operations after Plt Off Walton, in Spitfire IX MK426/SK-D, had flown its last patrol. The Tempest Vs remained in the vanguard of anti-V1 operations, however, and early on the morning of the 9th No 486 Sqn's Flt Lt Harvey Sweetman had his penultimate success – despite his cannon fire hitting a wing and shooting off the engine, the V1 stubbornly continued to fly, eventually crash-landing near Hastings!

The Spitfire XIIs of No 41 Sqn, which flew from several airfields (including Lympne, seen here), played an important part in the campaign. The nearest aircraft is MB854/EB-Z, which was used by Flt Lt Ross Harding to claim one of his three V1 kills. Behind it is MB856/EB-X in which Flt Lt Terry Spencer shot down his first V1 on 23 June (*via I Simpson*)

The next day the Belgians began operations, flying 23 sorties against V1s as their CO, Sqn Ldr 'Mike' Donnet, later recalled;

'We had sufficient speed to catch them, and one of our pilots on one occasion, having exhausted his ammunition without destroying the thing, flew alongside and, carefully judging his distance, managed to tip its wing and upset its gyroscopic control device.'

He was not, however, particularly enamoured with the flying bomb;

'We did not like these new weapons. We could face any human enemy, but these new soulless, mechanical menaces – nasty and anonymous, which arrived like a comet leaving a long, red glaring tail behind them – were different.'

Also newly equipped with the Griffon-engined Spitfire was Canadian-manned No 402 Sqn under eight-victory ace Sqn Ldr Wilbert Dodd. The unit flew its first operations at noon on 10 August, with patrols in the Ashford area. One V1 was attacked by Flt Lt de Niverville but without success. No 616 Sqn's Meteor Is had better luck, as its ORB Sqn described;

'Flg Off Dean completed his hat trick when he shot down a "Diver" near Ashford with two short bursts of his cannon. Flg Off Moon, who was with Flg Off Dean, saw the "Diver" sent spinning to earth.'

These successes made 'Dixie' Dean the top scoring jet pilot against the V1.

No 501 Sqn's erstwhile colleagues in No 274 Sqn also began operations on 12 August, with their outgoing CO, Canadian ace Sqn Ldr Eddie Edwards, managing a few sorties before departing, albeit without any success. In fact there were no daylight claims over the next three days, leading to hopes that the crisis might have passed. Sadly, the squadron lost its first aircraft on 13 August when Flt Sgt Ryman crashed in bad weather

Several senior officer aces managed to get attached to operational units during the V1 campaign, among them Wg Cdr Joe Fraser, who was attached to No 274 Sqn. On 17 August he used this Tempest V (EJ644/JJ-G) to claim his only flying bomb victory (*via T Buttler*)

and was killed. No 274 Sqn achieved its first V1 victory on the 15th when Flt Lt Willis claimed the first of three he would shoot down. That same day the Belgians in No 350 Sqn also shot down their first V1, while future ace WO Pat Coleman of No 41 Sqn claimed his second. Five minutes after Coleman's success, No 306 Sqn's WO Witold Nowoczyn used his Mustang III to shoot down his fifth 'Diver' near the unit's airstrip at Brenzett. Having set its power unit on fire, he saw it crash just west of Ashford.

Flying as a supernumerary with No 274 Sqn during August was Wg Cdr Joe Fraser, who had become an ace in Gladiators over Greece three years earlier. Having completed a number of uneventful 'Diver' patrols, he at last spotted a V1 on the 15th. However, as Fraser closed on it the missile hit barrage balloons and crashed near West Malling. The next day he noted in his log book that another 'Diver' he was chasing 'crashed just before opening fire'. The log book then notes further sorties on 16 August;

'Tempest F – AA destroyed three, chased fourth to Maidstone.

'Tempest G – fired three bursts with hits only, Meteor destroyed. Chased second, one Diver destroyed east of West Malling.'

Fraser was not the only ace to have been frustrated by the balloon barrage, as No 616 Sqn's ORB for 16 August noted;

'23 sorties flown – 2 Divers destroyed – Flg Off W McKenzie near Maidstone and Flg Off Mullenders (Belgian) near Ashford. CO had bad luck. Intercepted 2 Divers northwest of Tenterden and attack made from astern. Closing to 300 yards, saw strikes, Diver slowed up but Wing Commander had to break away owing to balloon barrage and so was unable to observe the end of the Diver's flight. Second was attacked near Tenterden, and again after recording strikes Wg Cdr McDowall forced to break away on reaching the balloon barrage without observing results. Two V1 claimed as damaged.'

Among the Mosquito nightfighter units committed to anti-'Diver' operations was the Australian-manned No 456 Sqn at Ford. One of its flight commanders was nightfighter ace Sqn Ldr Geoff Howitt, seen here getting out of Mosquito XVII HK249/RX-B in which he shot down two V1s during August (*via J W Bennett*)

Like Joe Fraser, Wg Cdr 'Paddy' Woodhouse was another successful pilot attached to a frontline ADGB fighter unit for experience of V1 operations. The five-victory ace was seconded from No 51 Operational Training Unit to No 85 Sqn, and had shot down two V1s by the time he was killed in a takeoff accident in a Mosquito on 13 August.

That same night No 456 Sqn's Australians successfully engaged V1s as they came over the Channel, shooting down three. One was credited to flight commander Sqn Ldr Geoff Howitt, who had achieved six victories flying Havoc Is and Mosquito XIIs with No 85 Sqn during two tours in 1940/41 and 1942/43. Flying his regular Mosquito XVII HK249/RX-B, Howitt's second, and last, V1 blew up in front of him, damaging the leading edge of his port wing just outboard of the engine.

The previous week Howitt's fellow flight commander, Sqn Ldr 'Bas' Howard, had shot down a pair of V1s. He would subsequently become No 456 Sqn's second 'Diver' ace before the end of August. Howard was also the last pilot to achieve this accolade flying the Mosquito, although other aces were to claim V1s when flying the de Havilland aircraft, among them Flt Lt Alfred Marshall of No 25 Sqn. One of the leading Hurricane pilots from the desert war, he was airborne on an anti-V1 patrol before dawn on 16 August when he encountered flying bombs heading for southeast England;

'As Flg Off Allen and I patrolled south of the South Foreland at 8000 ft I saw three flying bombs coming – two at 8000 ft and the other at about 2000 ft. At 0530 hrs I saw another at 2000-3000 ft travelling at about 360 mph. I dived and attacked, opening fire from approximately 300 yards. After the first burst the radar went u/s and it was difficult to judge range. As I turned away, I saw the flying bomb explode in the air.'

It was Marshall's only V1 claim. Earlier that night squadronmate Flt Lt Len Harvey shot down two, and although he was to bag another during September, frustratingly, a fifth V1 success eluded him.

This Mustang III of No 315 Sqn is thought to be FX995/PK-E, in which V1 ace Flt Sgt Kazimierez Siwek claimed 2.5 of his successes. Other notable pilots who shot down flying bombs in this fighter were Flt Lt Franciszek Wiza (three victories over aircraft) and WO Ryszard Idrian (four victories over aircraft) (*PI and SM via Wojtek Matusiak*)

Two hours after Marshall's success, No 130 Sqn, newly re-equipped with Spitfire XIVs, achieved its first V1 kill when Flg Off Jones sent one down in flames near Rochester. No 402 Sqn also opened its V1 account when Flg Off Ed Vickers spotted one off Cap Griz Nez and attacked it over the Channel, although the missile actually came down close to the unit's Hawkinge base! The 16th was a significant day for No 3 Sqn too, as during the evening its leading V1 scorer, Flt Lt Remi van Lierde, shot down his final missile to take his total to 44, nine of which were shared. Also making his final claim was No 486 Sqn's top scorer, WO 'Ginger' Eagleson. Flying over the coast near Rye, the New Zealander brought down three to take his total to 20 and three shared. He later described how he destroyed one of them in a somewhat unusual manner;

'I was under control of a ground station and was being directed onto a bomb. I came down through cloud from about 5000 ft and broke through at 3000 ft. Control told me that I should be alongside the bomb, but I could not see it. Finally, I looked behind and there it was right on my tail. I pulled away violently and my slipstream flicked it over onto its back, the bomb crashing into a field six miles north of Rye.'

The most successful unit on 16 August was No 274 Sqn, which brought down seven V1s, including two to Flt Lt Malloy and another to Flt Lt Willis, who was to end the campaign as the squadron's most successful pilot with three destroyed.

Unusually, there was no activity overnight, and the 17th showed the marked reduction in intensity of the bombardment. It did, however, see No 616 Sqn's jets have their most successful day, shooting down three V1s, the first falling to Canadian Flg Off Jack Ritch, who, having fired on it from about 150 yards astern, saw the missile roll over and explode when it hit the ground near Maidstone. That night there was again reduced activity, with just 12 V1s being brought down. Only one of these fell to a nightfighter, and just six were claimed by fighters during daylight hours on the 18th. One of the latter was credited to No 129 Sqn Mustang III pilot Flt Lt Desmond Ruchwaldy, who shot down a V1 over the coast near Boulogne soon after it had launched. This victory gave him 'dual' ace status, as he had previously shot down seven German aircraft.

There was renewed activity for the fighters on the night of 18/19 August, with five V1s being brought down, including two by No 605 Sqn's Flt Lt Brian Williams to make him the unit's final 'Diver' ace. Having spotted a gaggle of eight V1s over the French coast, he gave one a short burst and it exploded. He then went after another. 'Attacked again from astern and slightly above, and after two bursts Diver blew up at 0327 hrs about eight-ten miles northwest of Le Touquet'.

Williams' success presaged a lot more activity after dawn on 19 August. Among the successful pilots was No 129 Sqn's Flg Off Jim Hartley, who shot the starboard wing off a V1 to move his total on to nine. In the evening his squadronmate WO Eric Redhead shot down his final 'Diver', giving him V1 ace status. Up from Manston, No 616 Sqn's Meteor I pilots added to their tally by bringing down two missiles, with a third being shared. That night, AA again brought down the bulk of the flying bombs destroyed. However, two did fall to ADGB fighters, the first being claimed by Flt Lt 'Monty' Burton of No 501 Sqn – he would become a V1 ace later in the year.

All four of these pilots from No 315 Sqn found success against the flying bombs. They are, from left to right, WO Tadeusz Slon (one and two shared destroyed) and Flt Lts Michal Cwynar (two and four shared destroyed) and Jerzy Schmidt (two and two shared destroyed). In the foreground is the squadron's leading V1 ace, Flt Sgt Tadeusz Jankowski (four and six shared destroyed) (*PI and SM via Wojtek Matusiak*)

Although the rate at which V1s were being fired at southern England had by now significantly decreased, flying bombs continued to fall on London. Indeed, 11 civilians were killed by one missile at Feltham at lunchtime on the 20th just as people were returning from their Sunday worship.

No 501 Sqn's CO, Sqn Ldr Joe Berry, had sortied early that day, and at 0630 hrs he brought down his penultimate V1 while flying over central Kent. Also airborne on 19 August was Flt Sgt Paul Leva of No 350 Sqn, who, many years later, described how he claimed his unit's final 'Diver';

'I climbed as quickly as possible to a nice comfortable altitude from where, in principle, I would be able to dive on any bomb passing underneath me. Soon after the familiar voice of the controller came on, telling me that a flying bomb had been spotted on the radar, and he gave me its position and heading. Soon, with my speed dropping after levelling off, I could see that the distance separating us had not diminished. Indeed, it had even begun to increase. Utterly disappointed, I nevertheless opened fire, aiming high to compensate for the distance. I had the happy surprise to see some impacts and bits flying off the wings.

'I fired burst after burst, damaging the bomb still more. Although no vital part was hit, its speed diminished and it entered into a shallow dive. My hopes were soaring again. I was now approaching my target so fast that I had to throttle back. Ready for the kill, I positioned myself at what I estimated was the right distance. I depressed the trigger, but instead of the staccato of firing bullets I heard only the sound of escaping compressed air.

'It was then that I suddenly remembered the briefing we had received about sending V1s out of control by tipping up one wing. Adjusting the throttle, I eased myself forward until I came abreast of the bomb. What

The ubiquitous NAAFI wagon at No 41 Sqn's dispersal at Lympne allows hard working groundcrews to 'take five' with 'tea and a wad'. In the background is Spitfire XII MB882/ EB-B in which Flt Lt Terry Spencer shot down his fifth V1 on 23 August (*No 41 Sqn Records*)

a sight at close range! The wings were so ragged with the impacts of bullets that I wondered how it could still fly almost straight and level. Positioning myself slightly underneath, I placed my starboard wingtip under the port wing of the bomb. I came up slowly, made contact with it as softly as I could and then moved the stick violently back and to the left. This made me enter a steep climbing turn and I lost sight of the bomb. As I continued turning fast through 360 degrees I saw it well below me, going down steeply, hitting the ground with a blinding flash.'

Several hours later Flg Off Ray Clapperton of No 3 Sqn claimed his last 'Diver' to take his tally to 24. This score was good enough for him to be placed fifth in the table of V1 aces.

Further flying bombs fell the following day, with almost 50 losing their lives despite the AA gunners in particular continuing to exact a heavy toll on the V1s. The only one shot down by fighters on the 21st was significant, however, in that it was credited to Wg Cdr Beamont as his final 'Diver' claim. His tally of 26 and five shared destroyed placed him fourth in the list of high-scoring V1 aces.

Sadly, the cost of this success continued to mount for the ADGB later in the day when, having got airborne in bad weather, Flt Lt Cyril Thornton died when his Tempest V hit the ground near Woodnesborough, in Kent, whilst trying to descend through thick fog. He had fallen victim to the expendability policy that No 501 Sqn had been ordered to observe.

Other pilots continued to achieve ace status against the V1, including Flt Lt Terry Spencer of No 41 Sqn. He shot down two V1s on 23 August, the first of which not only took him to this milestone but also saw his unit achieve its half-century;

'Saw "Diver" at 4000 ft. Closed in and fired, no strikes seen until second bursts, when strikes seen on port side and wing. Petrol tank exploded and "Diver" flicked over and went in.'

When the flying bomb came down it blocked a railway line and damaged a number of houses near Harrietsham, in Kent. Other Griffon-engined

With eight V1s destroyed, Flt Lt Terry Spencer was No 41 Sqn's leading 'Diver' ace. He later commanded No 350 (Belgian) Sqn (*No 41 Sqn Records*)

Spitfires were also in action that day too, with No 130 Sqn bringing down V1s in the morning. One of them fell to Sgt Peter Standish, whose second burst of fire blew off the bomb's starboard wing. This success took his tally to four, but he would not get the opportunity to achieve his fifth.

That evening No 91 Sqn V1 ace Flg Off Ted Topham reverted to type (albeit now in a Spitfire IX) when, returning from a sweep to Abbeville, he spotted a flying bomb over the Channel and shot it down. It was one of 17 brought down on the 23rd. Like No 91 Sqn, within a few days the ADGB's remaining Spitfire XIV units (Nos 130, 350 and 402 Sqns) were stood down from anti-'Diver' patrols and returned to operations over the Continent.

With the coming of dawn on 24 August Tempest V pilots shot down three V1s. One of these fell to Flt Lt 'Spike' Umbers of No 3 Sqn as his final claim, while Flg Off 'Lulu' Deleuze of No 501 Sqn got his second success when he shared a 'Diver' with Flg Off Stockburn. The latter was to shoot down two more 48 hours later.

After recovering from his injuries, WO Jimmy Sheddan returned to the fray when, at 2040 hrs on 24 August, he destroyed his final V1. Shortly afterwards Flt Lt Wlodzimierz Klawe of No 306 Sqn, flying a Mustang III, shot down his final V1 too, having become an ace after destroying another earlier that same day.

Later that night No 96's CO, Wg Cdr Edward Crew, flew a Mustang III on two sorties to evaluate its use – he was eventually to fly seven sorties in FB379 over the next few weeks. Whilst he was conducting this unofficial trial, the remaining crews from his unit were up in Mosquitoes catching a number of flying bombs over the Channel. Flt Lt Don Ward shot down his 12th, and last, missile that night, whilst at dawn 'Togs' Mellersh cemented his place as the leading Mosquito pilot against the V1 by shooting down two more. Also shooting down a pair that night was No 456 Sqn's Flt Lt Keith Roediger, who despatched his last missiles within five minutes of each other to become the Australian unit's most successful pilot.

There was little action for the defending fighters on 25 or 26 August, the latter date only proving significant for the handful of fighter units visited by the ADGB C-in-C, Sir Roderick Hill, who flew in at the controls of his personal Tempest V.

Although now witnessing a marked reduction in 'Diver' activity, the night of 26/27 August saw several notable engagements. Shortly before 0200 hrs on the 27th Flt Lt John Musgrave of No 605 Sqn, still flying with Flt Sgt F W Samwell, spotted two V1s off Boulogne;

'We were flying at 7000 ft, and when Diver was well clear of French coast, dived to attack and gave in all six bursts of cannon and machine gun fire.'

Musgrave saw many hits all over the missile before the engine spluttered and it exploded. The crew that almost ten weeks earlier had destroyed the first V1 of the campaign had now shot down their 12th, and last, flying bomb. A little later No 96 Sqn's 'Togs' Mellersh shot down his penultimate flying bomb, but the bulk of the night's victories fell to No 501 Sqn, and most unusually there was no claim for its CO! The honours undoubtedly belonged to young New Zealander Flt Lt 'Snowy' Bonham, whose bravery had earned him the DFC whilst flying Buffaloes over Malaya in 1941/42 – he had been badly wounded during this ill-fated campaign.

Shortly after dawn on the 27th Bonham had brought down four V1s, although only one of these was distroyed with cannon fire. Having exhausted his ammunition downing the first 'Diver', he claimed the remaining three by 'tipping' their gyro guidance systems with the wingtip of his Tempest V. Bonham is believed to have been the only pilot to down three V1s in a single mission by tipping. If this sortie had not been eventful enough, the New Zealander was then forced to make a deadstick landing when he ran out of fuel. Once on the ground, he calmly called his squadron at Manston and arranged for some fuel to be brought over! Bonham's squadronmate Flg Off Bill Polley also brought a 'Diver' down during this mission, his claim elevating him to V1 ace status.

With the day fighters taking up the strain, an hour or so later No 3 Sqn's Plt Off 'Dickie' Wingate brought down his last V1, as did No 486's Flt Lt Jimmy Cullen, who took his score to 14 and four shared. Also shooting down his final V1 was Flg Off Bill MacLaren, who thus became No 56 Sqn's fifth, and last, V1 ace. No 501 Sqn gained another V1 ace just before dawn the following day when 'Snowy' Bonham shot down his fifth, and last, 'Diver' near Rye.

Although the campaign was perceived to be running down, almost 100 flying bombs were to be launched against Britain during the course of 28 August. Fighters shot down 25 of them, and only four reached London. The day's action was witnessed by the C-in-C of ADGB, who was airborne once again in his Tempest V. 'The whole was as fine a spectacle of cooperation as any commander could wish to see'. Among those that claimed was No 3 Sqn's Flt Sgt Bob Cole, who shot down his final two V1s to take his tally to 23, whilst Flt Lt Terry Spencer shot down No 41 Sqn's last flying bomb. Another pilot claiming in a Griffon-engined Spitfire was Flg Off Pat Bangerter, who shot down two 'Divers'. The biggest bag though went to No 129 Sqn, whose Mustang III pilots brought down eight – two of these fell to Flg Off Jim Hartley and another to fellow V1 ace Flt Lt 'Dutch' Kleinmeyer for his final success.

29 August was also a busy day, and again only a handful of 'Divers' reached their target. AA batteries claimed almost 60 destroyed and fighters a further 25. No 3 Sqn was credited with its last V1, this success providing Flt Sgt Bob Barckley with his 13th victory. No 486 Sqn shot down four and shared a fifth, with V1 aces Flg Offs Ray Cammock, Keith Smith and Bev Hall and Plt Off Jack Stafford all making their last claims. Four more were downed by No 274 Sqn, including one by Flt Lt David 'Foob' Fairbanks, who would later become the most successful Tempest V pilot in terms of aerial victories. He had a close call, as the unit diary noted. 'One moment Fairbanks was firing at his nimble target, the next instant he was flying in the midst of its flaming debris'. The explosion severely damaged his Tempest V.

Also making his final claim was Polish pilot Flt Lt Andrzej Beyer of No 306 Sqn, his victory being enough to make him the last Mustang III pilot to become a V1 ace. That same day Flg Off Pat Bangerter of No 610 Sqn achieved this distinction too, becoming the last pilot to 'make ace' in a Spitfire. No 616 Sqn's Meteor Is also made their final claim when, in the early afternoon of 29 August, Flg Off Hugh Miller shot a V1 down near Sittingbourne. It was No 129 Sqn that was again the most successful unit on this date, with Flt Lt Desmond Ruchwaldy downing four. He ended his V1-hunting career in spectacular style by 'tipping' the last one into the sea off Dungeness after his guns had jammed. Squadronmate Flg Off Jim Hartley also shot one down to take his total to 12 – a score that made him the most successful V1 hunter in the Mustang III.

After this period of intense action, V1 activity during the last two days of August was much reduced. Nevertheless, during the night of the 30th No 456 Sqn's Sqn Ldr 'Bas' Howard downed a pair of 'Divers', thus making him the last of 33 pilots to become V1 aces flying the Mosquito. Having exploded one missile, he then described in his Combat Report how he shot down his fifth V1;

'Saw "Diver" south of Gris Nez above cloud at 6000 ft climbing slightly. I penetrated tops of clouds to find flying bomb just on tail, so dropped back to 1200 ft and, from dead astern, fired three bursts. Strikes seen each time and flames changed colour. Shower of sparks. Light went out and it glided down very slowly and exploded in sea.'

There were a few additional claims on 31 August, the last, in mid-evening, by WO Brian O'Connor, giving the New Zealander his tenth victory. This also proved to be No 486 Sqn's 241st, and last, success of the anti-'Diver' campaign, making it the second most successful unit after No 3, which was credited with around 300 V1s destroyed.

Earlier that day, the most successful 'Diver' ace of them all had made his 61st, and final, claim, Sqn Ldr Joe Berry writing;

'I saw a Diver in the Sandwich area at 3000 ft and 250 mph. I closed in to 3000 yards dead astern and fired a short burst, which knocked pieces off the propulsion unit. I fired again from 150 yards and saw more strikes. The Diver exploded on the ground in the Faversham area.'

Although more missiles would continue to be launched against England, the crisis had passed.

AIR-LAUNCHED OFFENSIVE

On 16 May 1944 the Chief of the German High Command had issued Hitler's Directive for the bombardment of London, principally using the FZG 76 (V1). Significantly, among the weapons specified was 'FZG 76 launched from He 111' that was intended to supplement the bombardment of *Flak-Regiment* 155 (W) and enable attacks to be made on cities outside the range of land-based launch sites.

During spring 1944 III. *Gruppe* of *Kampfgeschwader* 3 (III./KG 3) had been recalled to Germany from the Eastern Front to convert to the Heinkel He 111H-22, which had been converted to enable the air-launching of a V1 flying bomb. The Heinkels had the bomb racks and ventral gun position removed, the underside of the starboard wing root strengthened and heavy lugs fitted to enable the carriage of a V1 that weighed some 4700 lbs. The tactic required the He 111 to fly at extremely low level to avoid detection until, on approaching the launch point off the British coast, the bomber would sharply increase its altitude to about 1500 ft and accelerate to around 180 mph, before releasing the V1 in the general direction of the target city. It would then descend back to low level and, wherever possible, use cloud cover to return to base.

After a lengthy period of training on the Baltic coast the *Gruppe* moved forward to Venlo, in Holland, to commence Operation *Rumpelkammer*, launching its first V1 against London on the night of 7/8 July. Initially, the campaign was seen as being successful, with III./KG 3 launching several hundred missiles in July and August against London, Portsmouth and Southampton, as well as a few against Bristol and Gloucester. This initial success prompted the Luftwaffe to convert more than 100 He 111Hs and to expand air-launched V1 operations to full *Geschwader* strength. Thus, in August, KG 53 was withdrawn from Russia to convert to the role too, absorbing III./KG 3 in the process.

As events were to prove, however, this initial success was a Pyrrhic victory. In addition to the hazards of the launch, and having inexperienced crews, the He 111s were to prove extremely vulnerable to the RAF's formidable night defences – especially when the launch illuminated the aircraft for several seconds. As a result, KG 53 suffered crippling losses during the autumn and early winter of 1944. One Heinkel pilot ruefully recalled;

'We were instructed how to fly a set course over the sea in order to launch the V1, which was attached to the underside of the bomber. With the V1 attached the Heinkel's performance was of course weakened. We flew over the North Sea for some distance before igniting the V1's motor and releasing it. The things could be a positive menace as they did not always fly true, and we felt in great danger with the contraption beneath us.'

With the final break out from Normandy in mid-August and the rout of the German 7th Army, the sweeping advance of British and Canadian

During the last months of 1944 the flying bomb bombardment of English cities was sustained by He 111Hs modified to air-launch V1s. Initially flown by III./KG 3 and then by KG 53, units operating these aircraft suffered heavy losses (*via John Weal*)

troops across the Pas de Calais saw the evacuation of V1 launching units to new sites in Holland. This move seriously affected the number of flying bombs launched, and resulted in the offensive petering out quite quickly.

On 1 September No 129 Sqn's CO, former Malta ace Sqn Ldr Peter Thompson, flying Mustang III FB123/DV-H, shot down his second V1. Minutes later, squadronmate WO Tommy Hetherington claimed the unit's 66th, and last, 'Diver'. The latter was also the last V1 shot down by the dedicated anti-'Diver' day fighter units. The missiles would continue to fall, but they now mainly emanated from He 111s. From February 1945, the Germans were able to ground-launch the long-range Fi 103E from newly-constructed sites in Holland.

No 129 Sqn and its Polish counterparts subsequently transferred to long-range escort duties, while the Tempest V and Spitfire XIV squadrons joined 2nd TAF on the Continent. No 501 Sqn, however, remained with the ADGB, moving to Bradwell Bay, in Essex, on 22 September to operate alongside Mosquito squadrons based in East Anglia that had been charged with covering the new Holland-based V1 threat axis.

However, the end of the main V1 assault on England merely presaged a new horror – the V2 rocket, the first of which fell on London on 8 September. There was no obvious way to defend London from this weapon, save to attack the rocket's mobile launchers that were sited in northwest Holland. Frustratingly, this area remained in German hands until the end of the war.

LOW FLIERS

The RAF quickly became aware of the use of the V1-launching He 111s, and patrols to intercept them began in August. Among those thus engaged was Sqn Ldr Ben Benson of No 157 Sqn. His navigator, Flt Lt Lewis Brandon, described some of the difficulties encountered when chasing the low-flying bombers in a Mosquito;

'We were sent on a low-level patrol off the Dutch islands. If we could shoot down the Heinkel before it launched its toy, so much the better. We had two long and difficult chases of aircraft, both of which turned out to be Mosquitoes. We then saw what we thought must be a launching some way off. No AI [Airborne Interception radar] contact appeared, however. Again, we saw a launching some way from us but had no joy when we investigated. We returned home tired and rather dejected.'

The regular launches by the Heinkels, whilst nowhere near as intense as the land-based offensive of previous months, kept the defenders on their toes. For example, on 5 September No 501 Sqn's Flt Lt Keith Panter and Flg Off 'Lulu' Deleuze each shot one down. Panter was to be one of a number of pilots who destroyed four V1s, only for the all-important fifth one to prove elusive. There were only occasional intercepts until 16 September, when, soon after dawn, Flt Off 'Bud' Miller was airborne in a Tempest V from Bradwell Bay after contacts had been reported north of Felixstowe;

'I climbed to 7000 ft and saw a Diver coming in on a course of 285 degrees at 2500 ft at 340 mph. I dived down on it, closed in from 500 yards astern and opened fire. I saw strikes on the tail unit. Control told me to break off the engagement and I did so. I saw the Diver losing height and crash and explode on the ground near RAF Castle Camps 30 seconds after my attack at 0606 hrs.'

Two minutes later Miller spotted another V1 over his home airfield, and firing from astern, he caused it to explode in mid-air.

On most evenings as dusk fell He 111s continued to take off from their bases in northern Germany such as Varelbusch, Leck, Husum and Eggebeck, in Schleiswig-Holstein. A significant number were lost in crashes probably due to the inexperience of the crews involved. However, late on the night of 24 September, the first He 111H-22 was lost to the RAF when one was attacked by Flg Off Henley of No 25 Sqn. Although he only claimed a probable, Uffz Böhling's crew crashed upon returning to base. A few hours later Henley's CO, Wg Cdr Leicester Mitchell, was also credited with another 'probable' after a long chase in thick cloud, which had a base of just 700 ft, and heavy rain some 60 miles out over the North Sea;

The Tempest Vs of No 501 Sqn were active throughout the winter of 1944/45 against V1s fired from over the North Sea. Pilots flying EJ589/SD-J shot down six missiles, including one on the night of 23/24 October that provided future V1 ace Flg Off Don Porter with his first success. Nine nights earlier, on 14/15 October, Frenchman Flg Off 'Lulu' Deleuze had used EJ589 to shoot down two V1s to become a 'Diver' ace (*No 501 Sqn Association*)

The only USAAF pilot to become a V1 ace, albeit whilst serving with RAF units, was Flt Off 'Bud' Miller of Nos 605 and 501 Sqns (*No 605 Sqn via I Piper*)

'Bud' Miller shot down his ninth, and last, V1 whilst flying Tempest V EJ558/SD-R of No 501 Sqn from Bradwell Bay. It carried his score under the cockpit (*via C H Thomas*)

'I saw a flying bomb leaving the bogey, and this was observed on the AI. AI contact was obtained at four miles range on a "jinking" target. Range was closed on AI to 850 ft in thick cloud, and at 400 ft range a visual was obtained in a break in the clouds. A long burst from 800 ft produced strikes on the starboard wing root, and as the enemy aircraft disappeared into cloud the target was seen, with the aid of night glasses, by Flt Lt Cox to turn to starboard and go down. The combat took place at 1000 ft, and it is considered unlikely that the enemy aircraft could have pulled out from the dive before hitting the water. Greyfriars Control states that only one aircraft emerged from the combat.'

Nevertheless, Mitchell and Cox only claimed a 'probable', although He 111 wk-nr 8222/'5K+ES' of 7./KG 3 was indeed shot down.

The following night WO Len Fitchett of No 409 Sqn shot down another He 111, which blew up whilst over Holland en route to its launch point. Missiles were also intercepted, with Flt Lt 'Togs' Mellersh shooting down his last V1 – he and his navigator Flt Lt Michael Stanley intercepted the missile low over the sea, although when hit the flying bomb climbed to about 8000 ft in cloud, before crashing into the sea.

No 501 Sqn's Tempest Vs also remained active despite the weather, the unit's resident American, Flt Off 'Bud' Miller, shooting down his last 'Diver' on 25 September. His success was tempered by the death of fellow V1 ace Flt Lt Gordon 'Snowy' Bonham, who, having scrambled from Manston in bad weather, later radioed that he had a compass fault and was returning to base. Sadly, he crashed in Essex and was killed. Described as a superb and competent pilot by his peers, Bonham also had a reputation for being 'as mad as a hatter' and for possessing 'an almost cherubic smile'.

The next success against the low-flying He 111s fell to No 25 Sqn's CO when, shortly before dawn on the 29th, Leicester Mitchell again scrambled from Coltishall;

'On reaching the patrol position, I immediately saw a flying bomb being launched. I carried out a diving turn towards the flying bomb, at the same time informing Greyfriars Control, who in turn informed me of a bandit in the same position, turning to port. Losing height to 600 ft in a turn, contact was obtained at two-and-half miles range and 45 degrees to port, which I followed in a turn. Closing the range whilst at a height of just 200 ft, I obtained a visual at 1300 ft and identified a He 111. A short burst from 400 ft dead astern caused a violent explosion, and I was forced to make a hard climbing starboard turn to avoid debris that flew from the enemy aircraft. Turning back over the position of the enemy aircraft's crash, we saw flames on the sea, which continued to burn for two to three minutes.'

Their night's work was not done, however, for within a few minutes they were back in action;

'I saw a further flying bomb launched. I turned towards the flying bomb, losing height and informing Greyfriars Control of my bearing. I eventually obtained contact on a converging course. Waiting until the range closed to approximately one mile, I carried out a hard turn to port in order to close in behind the enemy aircraft, losing height to 150 ft and closing range rapidly. A visual was then obtained at 1500 ft range and identified with the aid of night glasses as a He 111. A short burst from 400 ft caused the port engine of enemy aircraft to burst into flames. Enemy aircraft lost height immediately and crashed in flames into the sea at 0545 hrs.'

Mitchell and Cox had brought down two aircraft from 9./KG 3, namely wk-nr 161726/'5K+AT' and wk-nr 8428/'5K+CT'. No 25 Sqn was to claim six more missile carriers over the next six weeks.

During September the fighter defences brought down just 19 V1s. However, with KG 53 now operating at full three-*Gruppen* strength, and the firing of some ground-launched missiles, there was a marked increase in activity during October. The month saw ADGB being retitled Fighter Command once again, and its fighters shot down 43 V1s and seven He 111s, with five more bombers being lost in crashes.

The CO of No 96 Sqn throughout the V1 campaign was Wg Cdr Edward Crew, who as well as being a leading nightfighter ace was also the second most successful nightfighter pilot during the anti-'Diver' operation (*AVM E D Crew*)

During the autumn campaign against the He 111 missile carriers, Edward Crew's allocated Mosquito XIII was MM446/ZJ-Y. Although he had no success in it, Flt Lt Kennedy did, sharing the destruction of a V1 with a Tempest V pilot from No 501 Sqn in the early hours of 29 September (*AVM E D Crew*)

One of No 501 Sqn's Tempest Vs, possibly EJ538, was stripped of its camouflage in an attempt to gain some additional speed. In October it acted as a backdrop for this 'team shot'. These men are, in the back row from left-right, unknown, Flg Offs Keith Panter (four V1s destroyed), Josef Maday RCAF (1.5 V1s destroyed) and Joe Johnson RCAF (four V1s destroyed), Flt Lt 'Monty' Burton (six V1s destroyed), Flg Offs Bob Stockburn, Bill Polley (six V1s destroyed) and Ron Bennett (four V1s destroyed) and unknown. In the front row, from left to right, are Pole WO Edward Wojczynski (three V1s destroyed), Capt Payne (Army Liaison Officer), Flt Lt Jackson Robb (13 V1s destroyed), Flt Lt Horry Hansen RNZAF, Sqn Ldr Alastair Parker-Rees (nine V1s destroyed), Flt Lts 'Ollie' Willis and Birks, WO S H Balam (one V1 destroyed), Flt Lt Tony Langdon-Down (2.5 V1s destroyed) and Flg Offs Jimmie Grottick (two V1s destroyed) and Harte (*No 501 Sqn Association*)

One of the first actions came on 1 October when No 96 Sqn's Wg Cdr Edward Crew used his borrowed Mustang III FB379 in an unsuccessful chase against a missile. Early the following day, in an attempt to interdict the V1-launching He 111s, Sqn Ldr Joe Berry led a trio of No 501 Sqn Tempest Vs on a 'Ranger' to attack them at their bases. On the return flight over Holland his aircraft was struck by light flak and he crashed to his death. It was a tragic blow for the squadron, which lost its charismatic and able CO. At the time of his death, Berry was by some margin the RAF's most successful V1 ace. He was replaced by another V1 ace, Sqn Ldr Alastair Parker-Rees, who was posted in from No 96 Sqn.

Operations continued nevertheless, and No 501 Sqn claimed its first V1 after Berry's death on 6 October, when 'Lulu' Deleuze destroyed one. The following day Flt Lt Leo Williams, at the controls of Tempest V EJ590/SD-L, shot down his fifth to emulate his erstwhile CO and become the latest V1 ace – he shot down another flying bomb four nights later. No 25 Sqn's Mosquitoes were also active, for on the night of 5/6 October a crew had brought down a He 111. The following evening 11 more heavily laden bombers took off and set course for their missile launch positions. Amongst those airborne from Coltishall to catch them was 17-victory ace Flt Lt Alfred Marshall of No 25 Sqn. East of Southwold he found a launch He 111, as he wrote in his report;

'Shortly after commencing patrol I saw a flying bomb released and soon afterwards my navigator obtained contact at one-and-a-half miles dead ahead at a height of 600 ft. I closed, obtained visual and identified a He 111. It was at 600 ft height, so I pulled up and opened fire with a two-second burst. An explosion occurred in the port wing and the aircraft disintegrated.'

Sadly, at the end of the month, Marshall lost his life in a flying accident.

As if losses to nightfighters were not enough, the night after Marshall's success He 111H-22 '5K+DS' collided with the mast of a navigation beacon near Petten, on the Dutch coast, whilst outbound and crashed, killing Fw Lothar Gall and his five-man crew. That same night another bomber fell to a No 25 Sqn Mosquito. Over the next two weeks, however, V1s continued to be intercepted. And some of those that got through still caused casualties, with 17 being killed in one incident.

Amongst the pilots to enjoy success during this period was No 501 Sqn's Leo Williams, who claimed two more V1s on successive nights. Matching his success on the 12th was squadronmate Flt Lt 'Jumbo' Birbeck, who also got one. The previous year he had flown the first operational sortie for a Griffon-engined Spitfire. On the night of 14/15 October, 'Lulu' Deleuze of No 501 Sqn became the last French pilot to become a V1 ace when he shot down two missiles – one of his kills damaged a public house when it crashed! Other established pilots also continued to claim V1s, among them Flt Lt Norman Head of No 96 Sqn, who, in the early hours of 16 October, flying Mosquito XIII MM460/ZJ-E with Flt Lt Andrews, shot down his seventh, and last, into the sea. The description of the three-and-a-half-hour-long sortie in his log book was precise and to the point. 'Patrol. Attacked flying bomb at 50 ft'. He noted the V1 victory with a swastika alongside the entry.

The bombers were difficult targets, however, as No 68 Sqn's CO, Wg Cdr George Howden, explained when, having got behind one, it launched its missile and the Heinkel immediately broke upwards;

'To avoid collision with flying bomb, I turned violently to starboard and dived. Flash and glow caused trouble in sighting. Visual contact lost and not regained.'

One of the difficulties for the RAF crews was that the He 111s cruised at 120 mph, which was slower than the stalling speed of the Mosquito. In an attempt to solve this problem, Fighter Command deployed Beaufighter VIFs against them. These machines were drawn from the Fighter Interception Development Squadron (FIDS), which had formerly been the FIU – crews assigned to the unit continued to use the old name, however. It was whilst flying one of the old 'Beaus' that Flg Off Desmond Tull claimed his last victory when, on the evening of 25 October, he shot down 2./KG 53's Ofw Hämmerle and his crew in He 111 '5K+ES'. Tull described how he went about destroying the bomber in his Combat Report;

'With moonlight slanting through scattered cloud at 2000 ft, about 60 miles east of Yarmouth, under Hopton GCI station control, we were given trade five miles ahead on a vector of 160 degrees. Almost immediately we established contact 20 degrees to starboard, range three-and-a-half miles. We followed and closed to 2500 ft, where a visual established and identified the target as a He 111. I pulled up dead astern at a range of 250 yards, height 700 ft, and fired a three-second burst. Strikes were seen and a shower of debris came back, followed by an opening parachute. The target was clearly illuminated by a concentration of red sparks, apparently caused by an explosion in the aircraft. I fired another burst of approximately four seconds. Strikes were seen and the target fell away to port in a violent spin. It hit the sea at 1945 hrs.'

Beaufighter VIF V8565/ZQ-F was one of two such machines used by the FIDS to counter the slow speeds of V1-launching He 111s. Flt Lt Jeremy Howard-Williams was at the controls of this aircraft when he shot a Heinkel down on 4 November. It was one of three He 111s destroyed by the FIDS' veteran nightfighters (*Sqn Ldr J N Howard-Williams*)

Another He 111 was damaged that night by a Mosquito XVII from No 125 Sqn, and on the morning of 31 October Sqn Ldr Bill Gill from the same unit went one better. Just before 0730 hrs, in conditions of low cloud and bad visibility, Gill and his navigator Flt Lt Haigh scrambled for an eventful sortie that lasted barely an hour, as the former vividly recounted;

'We were vectored at full speed towards "trade" in the east, eventually resulting in a contact flying at 600 ft some two-and-a-half miles from us. We turned hard and obtained the contact again – I had previously had a fleeting visual on a Heinkel 111 as it passed above us. We rapidly closed the range and I started to get fleeting visuals through the broken cloud. Opening fire, I gave the contact a long burst, which resulted in many hits on the starboard engine and fuselage. Many pieces flew off and the bomber started to go down steeply. I gave it a further burst and saw more hits on the tail, but then had to break away.

'The Heinkel went down to sea level, only to start climbing again for cover. I did a complete orbit and closed in rapidly. When I found it again the bomber was taking violent evasive action, despite its heavily smoking starboard engine. I gave it another long burst and saw many hits all along the starboard side of the fuselage that set it alight. The bomber then went straight down into the sea. From a quick glance there appeared to be no survivors.'

The pair had shot down He 111 'A1+BM' of 4./KG 53. They were then given urgent vectors to the northeast, and after a little while Haigh gained contact with another target that appeared out of a heavy rainstorm. Gill attacked and hit the He 111 with several bursts, stopping the port engine and apparently setting it on fire. After landing at Coltishall at 0830 hrs, he was credited with one destroyed and a second probably destroyed in his final air combat.

In late October 1944 the Fleet Air Arm's NFIU also sent a detachment of Firefly Is equipped with ASH radar to Coltishall to gain experience of night anti-V1 operations. The aircraft's first sortie was flown on the night of 25 October, when Lts J H Neale and J C Harrison took MB419 aloft. The NFIU flew occasional patrols for the rest of the year, but without any success. Neale did, however, optimistically open fire on a He 111 in cloud one night in December.

The V1-launching Heinkels were to suffer even heavier losses in November, with ten being shot down by nightfighters and 14 more destroyed by other causes. Clearly, such losses were unsustainable. The first fell victim to FIDS pilot Flt Lt Jeremy Howard-Williams in Beaufighter VIF V8565/ZQ-F. He encountered a bomber over the sea 45 miles east of Winterton-on-Sea, in Norfolk, on a cloudless, hazy, autumn evening, as he later described in a letter;

'On 4 November 1944, my navigator, F J MacRae, and I were lucky enough to be in the right place at the right time and we shot down a Heinkel, complete with its flying bomb, while it was in the acceleration stage at 1500 ft. I had lowered 30 degrees of flap for the interception on the climb, but the target was doing 140 mph when we caught up with it. Pilots from the resident Mosquito squadron reckoned that they could have done the same job at that speed, and there was some ill feeling about poaching. FIU got one more Heinkel this way, and then the Beaufighter was withdrawn to avoid further friction.'

This success was Howard-Williams' sixth claim, and third victory, and the He 111 was confirmed both by a Mosquito from No 125 Sqn and an air-sea rescue aircraft. The following night his flight commander, Sqn Ldr Bill Maguire, who in 1943 had scored five victories, claimed the last victory for the Beaufighter over England.

That same night (5/6 November) Flt Sgt Neal of No 68 Sqn brought down He 111 'A1+FN' of 5./KG 53, flown by Ofw Paul Flir, to claim his unit's first Mosquito victory. Interestingly, some of the Heinkels were targeting Portsmouth that evening. The mainly Czech-manned No 68 Sqn bagged another on 9/10 November, as did No 25 Sqn when Flt Lt Jim Lomas claimed the second of his three victories. Airborne the following night was squadronmate Flt Lt Douglas Greaves, a successful ace from the Mediterranean theatre. He described how, flying one of the new Mosquito XXXs in thick cloud, with tops at 6000 ft, he claimed his final, and the squadron's penultimate, victory;

'We were scrambled from Castle Camps at 0030 hrs on indications of Diver carrier activity over the North Sea. We patrolled under Bawdsey control at 5000 ft, and after an hour were told of some activity in our area. Shortly afterwards several Divers were seen at about 600 ft. We went down to 200 ft and obtained a contact at two-and-a-half miles 60 degrees off to port. We closed at 190 mph to 150 ft astern and slightly to port, obtaining a visual on a He 111 at 200 ft. We opened fire with a long burst from dead astern, and strikes were followed by a sheet of flame that was seen from the starboard engine and wing root. We climbed and saw the Heinkel, on fire, glide slowly to starboard and crash into the sea. The wreckage was still burning when we left for home.'

Crews from Nos 68 and 125 Sqns claimed two more He 111s that night.

Earlier in the month No 456 Sqn, now under the command of Wg Cdr 'Bas' Howard, had resumed anti-'Diver' patrols once again, but this time to counter the He 111s rather than the missiles themselves. By the end of November the unit had shot down two Heinkels, the first one falling to Flg Offs Doug Arnold and John Stickley on the 19th when

The night after Flt Lt Howard-Williams' success, his FIDS colleague Sqn Ldr Bill Maguire used a Beaufighter to shoot down He 111 wk-nr 700878/'A1+AC' of 4./KG 53. It was Maguire's sixth, and last, victory (*via C F Shores*)

A sight witnessed by several RAF nightfighter crews, as the unmistakable shape of a V1 is launched from a He 111 (*via B Ketley*)

they caught the bomber at 300 ft off the Suffolk coast just after it had fired its missile. Arnold then closed to about 100 yards and shot off three bursts, although return fire hit one of the Mosquito's propeller blades. The Heinkel's starboard engine started to burn just before the bomber crashed into the North Sea.

No 456 Sqn's second success came six days later on 25 November when He 111H-22 wk-nr 110304/'A1+BH' of 1./KG 53, still carrying a V1, was attacked at 0510 hrs ten miles off the Dutch island of Texel by Flg Offs Fred Stevens and Andy Kellett in Mosquito HK290/RX-J. Stevens remarked afterwards that it was 'the most exhausting 25 minutes flying I've ever had'. Sqn Ldr Bob Cowper, a six-victory nightfighter ace serving with No 456 Sqn, said of these operations;

'Chasing He 111s with their buzz bombs was the toughest flying test ever asked of us. They flew below our stalling speed, only feet off the water. Even after a lecture from me the night before, when I was Flight Commander of "B" Flight Mulhall and his observer killed themselves trying too hard.'

With the nightfighters active against the He 111s, No 501 Sqn's Tempest Vs continued to knock down some of the V1s launched by KG 53. One of the pilots to enjoy success during this period was Flt Lt 'Monty' Burton, who recounted his sortie on 23 November for the squadron's history;

Flg Off Fred Stevens of No 456 Sqn recorded his score of two He 177s and three V1s on the door of Mosquito XVII HK290/RX-J, which also proclaims its Aussie ownership! He later added an additional cross for the He 111 missile carrier that he shot down on 24 November (*via J W Bennett*)

'I particularly recall the one on the 23rd. That night it was very dark, with thick low cloud. I tracked a V1 at 700 ft and eagerly watched the light centring on the glass gadget [gunsight] – when the light became a central unit, I fired. Of course, I was far too close. The bomb exploded in my face and pieces of it hit my aircraft in various places. Worst of all, I was completely blinded by the explosion and couldn't see my instruments. I was at 200 ft flying at great speed, not knowing if I was going upwards, sideways or downwards! Eventually my sight returned and I flew back to base.'

Despite his traumatic experience, Burton had become the penultimate V1 ace.

It says much for the ability and persistence of the nightfighter crews that so many of the low-flying Heinkels were shot down, for they were never easy targets, as one frustrated Mosquito crew described;

'We were close behind for miles, but he was so close to the water that we just couldn't get at him without swimming. I closed in and spotted him. I could even see the thing hanging under the wing. But before I could fire, somebody lit the blue touch paper. There was a dirty great flash as the bomb went whooshing off on its way, and for the next five minutes I could see "sweet Fanny Adams". And that was that.'

On the evening of 5 December, KG 53's Heinkels launched 15 V1s, and of the seven missiles that reached the coast four fell to fighters, including one to No 501 Sqn's CO Alastair Parker-Rees for his only success in the Tempest V. Another was claimed by a Mosquito from his old unit, No 96 Sqn. This kill proved to be the unit's last, No 96 Sqn finishing the war as the fourth most successful ADGB squadron against the flying bomb.

Two nights later Flt Lts Porter and Langdon-Brown of No 501 Sqn were scrambled from Bradwell Bay after an inbound 'Diver' that they duly shot down between them. Flying Tempest V EJ605/SD-K, Don Porter not only claimed his fifth 'Diver' kill with his share of the claim, but also became the 155th, and last, pilot to become a V1 ace. Ten days later, on 17 December, his French colleague 'Lulu' Deleuze became the last V1 ace to destroy a flying bomb over the UK when he shot down his eighth, and last, flying bomb.

ANTWERP 'BLITZ'

As the Allied armies had advanced through Belgium and into Holland, the large Belgian port of Antwerp became a vital logistics hub to support their progress towards Germany. After the city had fallen undamaged to the 11th Armoured Division in early September, the enemy also recognised its strategic value. The following month it commenced a bombardment of Antwerp by V1s and V2s on the personal instruction of the *Führer* himself. The first rocket landed on 7 October, followed by the first V1s two weeks later. In six weeks almost 3000 had been launched against Antwerp and the city of Liege, which was also seen as a key Allied 'hub'.

With a huge arc of enemy-held territory within easy range of Antwerp, it was quickly evident that a system based on massed AA guns was the most effective form of defence. This meant that there was no need for an organised fighter screen as had been seen over England. The bombardment continued until the end of March 1945, killing more than 4500 civilians in the two cities.

Allied fighters of 2nd TAF and the USAAF's Ninth Air Force did encounter flying bombs on occasion, and naturally 'had a go'. By November the 422nd and 425th NFSs were based on the Continent at A-78, and during a routine patrol near Duren on the night of the 26th Lt Paul Smith, flying with Lt Robert Tierney, encountered a V1. Flying at 11,000 ft, they dived in their Black Widow 42-5544 *Lady Glen* after a missile. Flying at more than 400 mph, they closed the distance and opened fire – 20 mm rounds hit the engine pod. Keeping his distance, Smith fired another burst, causing the V1 to explode. He noted;

The last V1 to be shot down by the USAAF fell to 2Lt Melvyn Paisley of the 390th FS/366th FG, flying P-47D Thunderbolt 44-20545/B2-M, on 30 November 1944 (*M Paisley via J Scutts*)

The V1 was Melvyn Paisley's first air combat success, but he went on to be credited with four and two shared victories by war's end, including three in a single sortie on 1 January 1945 (*M Paisley via J Scutts*)

'The flaming debris fell into the clouds and there was a red glow as if the pieces of metal were glowing red hot.'

This was his first claim, and the only V1 credited to him, but by the end of the year Smith and Tierney had become an ace crew. Four days later another future ace, 2Lt Melvyn Paisley of the P-47D-equipped 390th FS/366th FG, shot down the last V1 to be claimed by the USAAF. Participating in his unit's first mission from Asch, in Belgium, Paisley had become separated in cloud from his section. He later recalled;

'As I broke out of the cloud cover an object caught my eye at "eight o'clock". It was low, maybe 2000 ft below me, steady on course and black as night. With a brisk "phut . . . phut . . . phut", the Jerry V1 buzz bomb sped on its course to England or maybe Antwerp. I shoved the throttle to the wall and went into a shallow dive, following close behind for 50 miles, plotting its course on my kneepad map. It was on a line towards Brussels.

'Surveying the area, I noticed there was mostly farmland ahead of the V1. I switched on the water injection and moved up on the V1, carefully placing my wing under its wingtip. The Doodlebug was much steadier than my "Jug", probably owing to the absence of a nervous pilot flying it. With a prodding right roll of my aileron, my "Jug" tipped the V1's right wing into the sky. Within seconds the V1 lost its brains and tumbled downward. Rolling back, I took a short blast at the black body as it fell, hoping to get a little camera coverage. What a stupid move that was. My plane lurched upwards as the V1 burst into the open field below – I barely escaped the explosion, which sent hoards of mud spurting into the air.'

Shortly thereafter Paisley downed his first manned aircraft, and on New Year's Day he was credited with four more in a single sortie. He received a DSC for this feat of airmanship.

Typhoon-equipped No 123 Wing was based at Gilze-Rijen, in Holland, the airfield being directly in the path of the flying bombs bound for Antwerp. The wing was led by New Zealand ace Grp Capt Desmond Scott, who recalled in his autobiography;

'Sometimes, after the day's work was over, I would take to the skies and try to shoot some of the V1s down. I would fly to meet them, and as they passed under me 3000-4000 ft below I would roll over, gain speed and dive after them. They were normally too fast for a Typhoon in level flight, and I had to let them get a good 200 yards ahead before opening fire, or the explosion could blow me up too. So, once they overtook me, I had little time to work with. I succeeded in blowing up only one in the air, but I sent several to earth, where they exploded.'

Typhoon ace and the commander of No 123 Wing, Grp Capt Des Scott, seen here in the life jacket, shot down three V1s over Belgium and Holland in December 1944, possibly when flying his personal Typhoon MN941/DJS (*Grp Capt D J Scott via C H Thomas*)

These are thought to have been the last V1s shot down by the Typhoon, as fighter engagements on the Continent remained the exception.

Catching KG 53's He 111s at their bases was also an effective counter. Shortly after 2000 hrs on 5 January 1945, Wg Cdr Russ Bannock, now commanding No 406 Sqn, encountered a stream of Heinkels that were taking off from Eggebeck, as he recalled afterwards;

'We turned hard and picked up the contact almost dead ahead, following it across the aerodrome. I dropped back and fired a one-second burst, and the enemy aircraft immediately burst into flames and spun into a wooded dispersal area.'

Bannock's victim was He 111H-16 wk-nr 162181/'A1+HT' of 9./KG 53, flown by the *Staffelkapitän* Hptm Jessen. Unaware of Bannock's presence, the Heinkels continued to take off on their V1-launching mission against London. Tailing another, Bannock closed on wk-nr 8187/'A1+CT', flown by Fw Schulz. However, before he could open fire the bomber suddenly yawed and crashed – whether this was due to the Mosquito's presence remains unclear. However, Bannock then unsuccessfully chased a third Heinkel, before damaging another one on the ground.

The last He 111 missile carrier to fall to a nightfighter was shot down on 5 January 1945 by a Mosquito XXX of No 406 Sqn flown by the unit's recently appointed CO, Wg Cdr Russ Bannock. Appropriately, he was a 'dual' ace against both V1s and aircraft (*RCAF*)

IMPROVED DETECTION

One of the recognised limitations of ground-based radar was its ability to detect low-flying aircraft at any range. One solution to this problem was to have an aircraft equipped with a search radar operated by a dedicated controller whose job it was to detect an intruder and then direct an intercepting fighter onto it. The FIDS, in conjunction with the Telecommunications Research Establishment (TRE), had conducted some studies in this area, and in late 1944 an ASV Mk VI radar-equipped Wellington was issued to the squadron for air intercept control. Trials had shown that when the Wellington was flying an elliptical orbit at an altitude of 4000 ft over the North Sea, its radar was able to detect a bomber at low level. Using this information, the controller was able to direct an intercepting fighter onto the contact.

After a period of training, the FIDS Wellington and Mosquito combination was ready to make its combat debut in January 1945. Codenamed Operation *Vapour*, the Wellington crew would set up an orbit at 4000 ft off the Dutch coast in formation with Mosquito nightfighters under control. Acting as the controller in the Wellington, flown by Flt Lt McLean, was TRE 'boffin' E J Smith. The main problem he found was identifying which of the detected 'blips' was a Heinkel, as Flt Lt Jeremy Howard-Williams, who flew one of the fighters, recalled;

'"E J" chose the firmest "blip" from the many on his tube. We were given the necessary vectors to get our own AI contact on the selected target, and this duly occurred. The target was flying slowly west, just as we had expected, and we settled down to an overtaking speed of 30 mph. Eventually we brought it to visual range and closed to identify. I could hardly believe my eyes – it was another Wellington! This was as near as anyone got. That night – 13 January 1945 – turned out to be the end of the Luftwaffe's air-launching effort.'

Howard-Williams' final comment was indeed true, as heavy losses and a critical shortage of fuel resulted in KG 53 being withdrawn from operations on 25 January. Whilst long-range Fi 103Es would continue to be fired at London from launch sites in Holland, the campaign was largely over.

To detect the low-flying missile-launching He 111s, the FIDS used an ASV radar-equipped Wellington XIII that carried an airborne controller to vector in attendant nightfighters. Unfortunately, the modified Wellington XIIIs arrived just as the He 111s were withdrawn from service (*L Hayes*)

CHAPTER SIX

THE LAST RITES

The withdrawal of KG 53 saw a lull in V1 activity against England for the first two months of 1945. The barrage against Antwerp and Liege continued, however, and sometimes 2nd TAF fighters encountered the V1s. During February Flt Lt Paddy Dalzell of No 74 Sqn, who had destroyed a V1 the previous June, shot down three more, thus narrowly missing out on becoming a 'Diver' ace. He recalled how, in his Spitfire LF IX, he brought one down over his base near Antwerp;

'I remember one day we were returning from an op over northern Holland at 2000 ft to land at Deurne, and a V1 overtook me about 30 yards on my starboard and on the same heading. As I had very little ammunition left, I tipped its wing and it went down into a field.'

Other tactical fighters also brought down flying bombs over the battle area throughout February. However, it was whilst flying from the UK on an intruder sortie in a Mosquito on the 27th that V1 ace Flt Lt Brian Williams unexpectedly brought down his sixth – his last claim had been the previous August! From time to time other V1 aces also claimed a kill. One such pilot was Flg Off Jan Jongbloed, who had shot down nine V1s with No 322 Sqn the previous summer but was now flying Tempest Vs with No 222 Sqn in Holland. On 28 February ten Tempest Vs led by the CO flew a sweep at 0800 hrs, the ORB noting that 'Flt Lt G F J Jongbloed clobbered a V1 with 20 rounds onto the southwest edge of the 'drome!'

When located, V1 sites in Holland continued to be attacked. For example, one at Ypenburg was hit on 20 February and another at Vlaardingen was targeted three days later. Nonetheless, in March 1945, 275 of the latest long-range V1s were fired at Britain from these ramps in Holland, although only 34 reached their targets. This 'mini-*blitz*' began on the 3rd, with most V1s being engaged by AA, although fighter patrols were also re-instituted.

HB861 wore some colourful artwork beneath the cockpit. This type of decoration was more usually seen on USAAF Mustangs (*PI and SM Archive via W Matusiak*)

On the afternoon of 6 March 1945, eight-victory ace Flt Lt Josef Jeka of No 306 Sqn encountered a V1 over Essex in Mustang III HB861/UZ-B and shot it down, thus claiming his only success against a flying bomb (*PI and SM Archive via W Matusiak*)

The last flying bomb shot down by Fighter Command fell to Flg Off Jimmie Grottick of No 501 Sqn on 25 March 1945 (*No 501 Sqn Association*)

Grottick was flying Tempest V EJ599/ SD-W when he claimed No 501 Sqn's final V1, this missile being one of four credited to the aircraft (*via T Buttler*)

On the afternoon of the 6th Flt Lt Josef Jeka of No 306 Sqn, flying a Mustang III, intercepted a 'Diver' near Maldon. Attacking from astern, the Polish ace opened fire and had the satisfaction of seeing the flying bomb crash into the ground. It was another Polish pilot, Flt Lt Stanislaw Blok of No 315 Sqn, who became the last ace to destroy a V1 when he shot down his only flying bomb during a patrol on the 24th. The last V1 to be brought down by Fighter Command fell, appropriately, to its 'expendable' unit No 501 Sqn. The pilot, Flt Lt Jimmie Grottick recalled;

'My second V1 was shot down on the night of 26 March 1945 when I was operating out of Hunsdon. It was an interesting kill, both for myself and No 501 Sqn. The V1 crashed and exploded near North Weald, and as far as I can ascertain I was the last pilot to down an intruder over Britain.'

It was not the last V1 shot down by a fighter, however. That distinction fell to No 409 Sqn's Flt Lt Martin Kent in the early hours of the 28th, the pilot gunning the missile down with his Mosquito near the Dutch town of Arnhem. The Canadian subsequently wrote in his report;

'We observed the launching of three salvos of four or five Divers. We immediately dived to attack, and closing slowly opened fire from 1000 ft dead astern. Strikes were observed and the engine apparently damaged, for the flame went out. The Diver went in and exploded on the ground at approximately 0115 hrs in the vicinity of Rheden. Shortly after, we attacked another Diver travelling at Angels 2. Strikes were again observed, some of which apparently hit the elevator, for the flying bomb immediately began to fly erratically, climbing and diving violently, before going on and exploding in the vicinity of Rade.'

The next day several V1s were launched from Delft, and the last to hit British soil struck Datchworth, in Hertfordshire, and another was shot down by AA fire and exploded in open country near Sittingbourne, Kent.

The terrifying V1 campaign was over. Of approximately 10,000 missiles fired at England, almost 2500 reached London and other cities, killing more than 6000 people and seriously wounding nearly 18,000 more. Of the defending pilots, no fewer than 155 had become V1 aces, with 25 of them also being aces against aircraft. Additionally, a further 35 RAF/Allied and nine USAAF aces made some claims against the V1.

APPENDICES

V1 ACES

Name	Service	Unit/s	V1 Victories	Aerial Victories
Berry J	RAF	FIU, 501	59+1sh	3/-/-
van Lierde R	Belg	3	35+9sh	6/-/1
Mellersh F R L	RAF	96	39 or 42	8/1/-
Beamont R P	RAF	150 Wg	26+5sh	9+1sh/2/4
Clapperton R H	RAF	3	24	-
Moore A R	RAF	3	23+1sh	4/1sh/-
Burgwal R F	Dutch	322	20+4sh	-
Eagleson O D	RNZAF	486	20+3sh	2+1sh/-/1
Cole R W	RAF	3	20+3sh	1+1sh/-/-
Kynaston N A	RAF	91	22	4+1sh/-/-
Wingate H R	RAF	3	19+3sh	
Crew E D	RAF	96	21	12+1sh/-/5
Cammock R J	RNZAF	486	20+1sh	-
McCaw J H	RNZAF	486	19+1sh	-
Slade-Betts K G	RAF	3	19+1sh	-
Nash R S	RAF	91	17+3sh	2+1sh/-/-
Bannock R	RCAF	418	18+1sh	9/4/-
Dryland R	RAF	3	17+2sh	1+1sh/-/-+1sh
Umbers A E	RNZAF	3	14+4sh	4+1sh/1+1sh/2+1sh
Cullen J R	RNZAF	486	14+4sh	-
Chudleigh R N	RAF	96	15	2/-/-
Johnson H D	RAF	91	13+1sh	-
Mackerras D J	RAAF	3	11+3sh	-
Bailey H G	RAAF	3	12+2sh	-
Green W P	RAF	96	13	14/-/-
Robb J L T	RAF	FIU, 501	13	1/-/1
Dobie I A	RAF	96	13	1/-/-
Barckley R E	RAF	3	12+1sh	-
Danzey R J	RNZAF	486	9+4sh	-/1/-
Ward D L	RAF	96	12	3/-/-
Hartley J	RAF	129	12	-
Musgrave J G	RAF	605	12	-
Rose M J A	RAF	3	11+1sh	2/-/1
Sweetman H N	RNZAF	486	11+1sh	1+2sh/1+1sh/-
Feldman S B	RAF (US)	3	9+3sh	1/-/-
Edwards M F	RAF	3	7+5sh	-
Williams E L	Rhod	FIU, 501	11	5 or 6/-/-
Plesman J L	Dutch	322	11	-
Cruickshank A R	RAF	91	10+1sh	-
Shaw H	RAF	56	8+3sh	2+3sh/-/-
Siekierski J	Pol	306	10	1/-/1
O'Connor B J	RNZAF	486	9+1sh	1/-/-
Topham E	RAF	91	9+1sh	-/-/1
Zalenski J	Pol	306	9+1sh	-
De Bordas H F	Fr	91	9+1sh	-
Newbery R A	RAF	610	8+2sh	3/2/-
Jongbloed G F J	Dutch	322, 222	8+2sh	1/-/1

Name	Service	Unit/s	V1 Victories	Aerial Victories
Rudowski S	Pol	306	7+3sh	2/-/1
Hooper G J M	RNZAF	486	7+3sh	1/-/1
Bond P M	RAF	91	7+3sh	-
Jankowski T	Pol	315	4+6sh	2+1sh/-/1
Whitman G A	RAF (US)	3	5+5sh	1/-/-
Parker-Rees A	RAF	96, 501	9	3/2/-
Miller B F	USAAF	605, FIU, 501	9	1/-/2
Roediger K A	RAAF	456	9	2/-/-
Thornton C B	RAF	FIU, 501	9	-
Ruchwaldy D F	RAF	129	8+1sh	7/3/6
Hall B M	RNZAF	486	6+3sh	-
Williams S S	RNZAF	486	7+2sh	1+1sh/-/-
Bremner R D	RNZAF	486	5+4sh	2sh/-/-
Stafford J H	RNZAF	486	8	2+3sh/-/-
Szymanski T	Pol	316	8	2/1/-
Smith K A	RNZAF	486	8	2/-/-
Spencer T	RAF	41	8	1/-/-
Bensted B G	RAF	605	8	-
Bryan J	RAF	96	8	-
Deleuze R C	Fr	501	8	-
Kalka W A	RNZAF	486	8	-
Moffett H B	RCAF	91	8	-
Wright G C	RAF	605	8	-
Siwek K	Pol	315	6+2sh	3/-/-
Balasse M A L	Belg	41	6+2sh	-
Hart W A	RNZAF	486	6+2sh	-
Janssen M J	Dutch	322	6+2sh	-
McLardy W A	RAF	96	6+2sh	-
Elcock A R	RAF	91	7+1sh	-
Kleinmayer R G	RNZAF	129	7+1sh	-
McPhie R A	RCAF	91	5+3sh	-
Sheddan C J	RNZAF	486	7+1sh	4+3sh/-/-
Head N S	RAF	96	7	4/2/-
Weisteen T	Nor	85	7	2/1/-
Marshall W C	RAF	91	7	2/-/-
Evans C J	RCAF	418	7	1+1sh/1/-
Collier K R	RAAF	91	7	-
Chisholm J H M	RAF	157	7	-
Miller W L	RNZAF	486	7	-
van Eedenborg C M	Dutch	322	7	-
van Arkel J	Dutch	322	6+1sh	1sh/-/1
Davy D H	RAF	1	6+1sh	1+2sh/-/-
Everson L G	RAF	3	6+1sh	-
Goode J	RAF	96	6+1sh	-
Mielnecki J A	Pol	316	6+1sh	-
Shepherd J B	RAF	610	5+2sh	8+5sh/1+1sh/2+1sh
Maridor J-M	Fr	91	5+2sh	3+1sh/2/3
Mason H M	RNZAF	486	5+2sh	-
Pottinger R W	RAF	3	4+3sh	+1sh/-/-
Parker G R I	RAF	219	6	9/1/1
Draper J W P	RCAF	91	6	4+1sh/2/1
Benson J G	RAF	157	6	10/-/4
Pietrzak A	Pol	316	6	3+1sh½/-/-
Cholajda A	Pol	316	6	2/1/2
Gough W J	RAF	96	6	2/1/-
Edwards E W	RAF	129	6	2/-/3

Name	Service	Unit/s	V1 Victories	Aerial Victories
Barllomiejczyk C	Pol	316	6	1/-/-
Caldwell G L	RAF	96	6	1/-/-
Trott W A L	RNZAF	486	6	1/-/-
Szymankiewicz T	Pol	316	6	1sh/-/-
Burton H	RAF	501	6	-
Lawson A M	RAAF	165	6	-
McCarthy K	RNZAF	486	6	-
Tinsey T D	RAF	165	5+1sh	3 or 4/1/1
Porteous J K	RNZAF	165	5+1sh	1/-/2
Majenski L	Pol	316	5+1sh	1sh/-/-
Wylde G H	RAF	56	5+1sh	-
Jonker J	Dutch	322	5+1sh	-
Klawe W	Pol	306	4+2sh	1/2/-
Osborne A F	RAF	129	4+2sh	1sh/-/-
Foster J K	RAF	3	4+2sh	-/-/1
Faulkner J A	RAF	91	4+2sh	-
Cwynar M	Pol	315	2+4sh	6+1sh/1/-
Swistun G	Pol	315	1+5sh	2+1sh/1/-
Matthews J O	RAF	157	5	9/-/6
MacFadyen D A	RCAF	418	5	7/1/-
Dredge A S	RAF	3	5	4/1/1+2sh
Hall A R	RAF	56	5	3/-/1
Brooke P deL	RAF	264	5	2 or 3/-/-
Howard B	RAAF	456	5	3/-/-
Sames A N	RNZAF	137	5	2+1sh/-/-
Beyer A	Pol	306	5	1+2sh/-/-
Bailey C A	RAF	FIU	5	2/-/-
Bonham G L	RNZAF	501	5	1/-/1
Nowoczyn W	Pol	306	5	1/-/1
Powell N J	RNZAF	486	5	1/-/-
Short S J	RNZAF	486	5	1/-/-
Williams B	RAF	605	5	1/-/2
Leggat P S	RCAF	418	5	-
May N S	RCAF	418	5	-
Neil H M	RAF	91	5	-
van Beers R L	Dutch	322	5	-
Walton R C	RAF	605	5	-
Oxspring R W	RAF	24 Wg	4+1sh	13+1sh/2/12
Bangerter B M	RAF	610, 350	3+2sh	2+2sh/-/-
Porter D A	RAF	501	4+1sh	2sh/-/-
McKinley G M	RAF	610	4+1sh	-
Redhead E	RAF	129	4+1sh	-
Pietrzak H J	Pol	315	4+1sh	7+2sh/1/1
Ness D E	RAF	56	4+1sh	5+1sh/-/-
Hastings I	RAF	1	4+1sh	-
Scamen B R	RCAF	610	4+1sh	-
Tanner E N	RNZAF	486	3+2sh	1/-/1
Karnkowski S	Pol	316	2+3sh	1+1sh/1/-
Horbaczewski E	Pol	315	1+4sh	16+1sh/11/
Maclaren W R *	RAF	56	4	3/-/-
Cramm H C*	Dutch	322	4	-
Polley W F*	RAF	501	3+1sh	-
Rogowski J*	RAF	306	3+1sh	2/-/-

Note

Those pilots with less than five victories are marked thus *, and are shown because of their inclusion in the authoritative volumes *Aces High* or *Those other Eagles*, or where there may be doubt as to their actual scores.

ACES WITH V1 CLAIMS

Name	Service	Unit/s	V1 Victories	Aerial Victories
Aanjesen D G	Nor	332	1	5+1sh/2/1
Bargielowski J	Pol	315	1+2sh	5/-/3
Barwell E G	RAF	125	1	9/1/1
Blok S	Pol	315	1	5/1/3
Boyd A D McN	RAF	219	1	10/-/1
Burbridge B A	RAF	85	3	21/2/1
Burke P L	RAF	219	2	5/1/1sh
Checketts J M	RNZAF	142 Wg	2	14/3/8
Coleman P T	RAF	41	2	5+2sh/-/-
Cosby I H	RAF	264	2	5+1sh/-/2
Cowper R B	RAAF	456	1	6/-/1
Daniel E G	RAF	FIU	4	7/-/1
Davison M M	RAF	264	1	12/1/1
Doleman R D	RAF	157	3	10+2sh/1/1+1sh
Edwards F E F	RAAF	130	1sh	2+4sh/-/1
Fairbanks D C	RAF	274	1	12+1sh/-/3
Fraser J F	RAF	274	1	9+1sh/-/2
Gaze F A O	RAF	610	1	11+3sh/4/5
Goucher R T	RAF	85	2	5/-/-
Harries R H	RAF	135 Wg	1	15+3sh/2/5+1sh
Hedgecoe E R	RAF	85	1	8/1/2
Howitt G L	RAF	456	2	6/1/1
Jasper C M*	RCAF	418	3	4/-/-
Jeka J	Pol	306	1	7+1sh/-/3
Kendall P S	RAF	85	1	8/1/2
LeLong R E	RNZAF	605	3	7/1/3
Lord G	RAF	130	1	5+1sh/-/1
Maguire W H	RAF	FIU	1	6/-/-
Mansfeld M J	Czech	68	2	8+2sh/-/2
Marshall A E	RAF	25	1	16+2sh/2/1
McDowall A	RAF	616	2 dam	11+2sh/2/- +1 on gnd
Miller C M*	RAF	85	1sh	4/-/-/ +2 on gnd
Nichols H T	RAF	137	1	6/1/3
Nowierski T	Polish	133 Wg	1	5/2/5+1sh
Owen A J	RAF	85	1	15/1/3
Payton J J	RAF	56	1	6/1/-
Powell P R P	RAF	Detling Wg	2	7+2sh/3/4
Raphael G L	RAF	CO Manston	2	7/1/1
Rayment K G	RAF	264	1	6/1/1
Schade P A	RAF	91	3+1sh	13+1sh/2/2
Scott D J	RNZAF	123 Wg	3	5+3sh/4+2sh/5+1sh
Singleton J	RAF	25	1	7/-/3
Smik O	Czech	310	3	8+2sh/2/3
Starr N J	RAF	605	1	5/1/2
Stephenson L	RAF	219	1	10/-/-
Taylor-Cannon K G	RNZAF	486	1	4+1sh/+1sh/-
Thompson P D*	RAF	129	2	1+3sh/1/3
Wagner A D	RAF	FIU	2	9/-/5
Wight-Boycott C M	RAF	25	2	7/-/2
Williamson P G K	RAF	219	2	9/-/1
Wilkinson J F	RAF	41	1	2+3sh/-/-
Woodhouse H deC A	RAF	51 OTU	1	3+2sh/-/4

APPENDICES

USAAF ACES WITH V1 CLAIMS

Name	Service	Unit/s	V1 Victories	Aerial Victories
Anderson W Y	USAAF	353rd FS/354th FG	1	7/-/-
Bickel C G	USAAF	353rd FS/354th FG	3	4+3sh/2/1
Dalglish J B	USAAF	355th FS/354th FG	3	8+2sh/-/6+1sh
Ernst H E	USAAF	422nd NFS	1	5/-/-
Fisher E O	USAAF	377th FS/362nd FG	3	7/-/-
Paisley M R	USAAF	390th FS/366th FG	1	4+2sh/-/-
Powers L H	USAAF	355th FS/354th FG	2+1sh	2+1sh/1/2+3 on gnd
Smith P A	USAAF	422nd NFS	1	5/-/-
Turner R E	USAAF	356th FS/354th FG	2	11/-/8

COLOUR PLATES

1

Tempest V JN862/JF-Z of Flt Lt R van Lierde, No 3 Sqn, Newchurch, June-August 1944

The first V1s to be shot down in daylight fell to No 3 Sqn on the morning of 16 June. The sixth fell to the guns of Flt Lt Remi van Lierde, flying this Tempest V. For the exiled Belgian pilot, who had become an ace when flying Typhoons the previous year, this victory was the first of 44 V1s that he would destroy (nine of which were shared) by mid-August. No fewer than 38 of them were claimed when he was flying JN862, which had three narrow bands around the spinner that may have been applied in the Belgian national colours of red, yellow and black. Like its pilot, JN862 survived the war. It was eventually sold for scrapping in 1950.

2

Mosquito VI HR155/TH-X of Flt Lt D A MacFadyen, No 418 Sqn RCAF, Holmsley South, June-July 1944

Canadian Don MacFadyen had already shot down three aircraft and destroyed many more on the ground as an intruder pilot when, in the early hours of 17 June, he encountered V1s for the first time. Flying this aircraft over the Channel with his navigator, Flg Off J D Wright, MacFadyen was patrolling at 10,000 ft when he spotted a missile being launched. Heading off to intercept it, the pilot put the Mosquito into a dive in order to increase the speed of the fighter. The V1 was soon destroyed, as was a second one engaged later that same evening. Success then eluded MacFadyen and Wright until 0100 hrs on 7 July when, again in HR155, the pair contributed to a bumper haul for No 418 Sqn by shooting down three 'Divers' to make the 23-year-old a V1 ace.

3

P-51B Mustang 43-6796/FT-T *Swede's Steed II* of 1Lt W Y Anderson, 353rd FS/354th FG, Lashenden, 17 June 1944

Flying from their Kent base in support of Allied troops in Normandy, the pilots of the 354th FG routinely saw V1s passing overhead on their way to London. At around 2000 hrs on 17 June 'Willie' Anderson was returning after a ground-strafing sortie in his P-51B 43-6796/FT-T *Swede's Steed II* when he spotted one of the flying bombs. He attacked and shot it down, thus claiming the destruction of the first V1

credited to the USAAF. After landing the 23-year-old asked, 'How many Doodlebugs make an ace?' Although this was his only encounter with a flying bomb, by early August Anderson had become an ace with seven aircraft to his credit.

4

P-47D Thunderbolt 42-26919/E4-E *Shirley Jane III* of 1Lt E O Fisher, 377th FS/362nd FG, Headcorn, 17 June 1944

The same evening as 1Lt Anderson claimed the first USAAF V1 victory, 1Lt 'Bill' Fisher was flying his massive P-47D back from a sortie over France when he spotted several 'Divers'. Within minutes he had shot down all three of them. Although this was his only engagement with flying bombs, Fisher became the USAAF's joint top scorer against them. He opened his account against aircraft a few weeks later after transferring with his unit to the Continent – within a month of the move he had become an ace with seven victories. Fisher named his aircraft after his wife.

5

Tempest V JN765/JF-K of Flg Off R H Clapperton, No 3 Sqn, Newchurch, 18 June 1944

One of the many V1 aces that flew with No 3 Sqn, Flg Off Ray Clapperton opened his account when flying this aircraft off Beachy Head shortly before midnight on 18 June. Having spotted a V1 flying at 2500 ft, he gave chase and closed to 400 yards, before firing two bursts that caused the missile to 'porpoise' and crash near Hailsham. This was the first of 24 V1s Clapperton would shoot down, but the only one he claimed in JN765 – other pilots were to claim eight V1s when flying it, however, including V1 aces Flt Sgt L G Everson and Plt Off Kenneth Slade-Betts. Sadly, JN765 crashed chasing a V1 on 1 July, resulting in the death of Flg Off George Kosh.

6

P-51D Mustang 44-13561/AJ-T of Maj R E Turner, 356th FS/354th FG, Lashenden, 18 June 1944

Returning from a dive-bombing mission on the morning of 18 June, Maj Dick Turner, CO of the 356th FS, was patrolling along the coast off Hastings in this aircraft looking for V1s when he spotted one and chased it for ten minutes. Failing to close on the missile, he opened fire in desperation and scored a lucky hit, causing the V1 to crash. Turner then resumed his

90

patrol and soon intercepted another missile. Diving on this one, he quickly exhausted his ammunition, but managed to formate on the V1 and tip it over with his wingtip. Turner's squadron moved to France later that day, from where he achieved his final three aerial victories. The V1s were the last successes Turner claimed in this particular aircraft.

7

Tempest V JN769/JF-G of Flt Lt A R Moore, No 3 Sqn, Newchurch, 19 June 1944

Having claimed the first of his four victories on 8 June, Moore downed his first V1 ten days later. Early the following evening (19 June) he was flying JN769 over Kent when he claimed his first 'double'. Firing on the first V1 near Rye, the No 3 Sqn flight commander saw the missile explode before crashing. A short while later Moore chased another 'Diver' for ten miles west of Hastings before hitting its tail. The V1 gradually lost height until it hit the ground near Tonbridge. Moore went on to claim a total of 23.5 V1s, for which he received a DFC. JN769 was also used by five other pilots to shoot down a further eight flying bombs.

8

Spitfire XII MB856/EB-X of Flt Lt T Spencer, No 41 Sqn, West Malling, 23 June 1944

With its high performance Griffon-engined aircraft, No 41 Sqn was quickly switched to the anti-'Diver' campaign. On 23 June, three days after it had bagged its first V1, the unit shot down three more, the last of them falling to Terry Spencer in MB856. Shortly after 2300 hrs, as dusk fell over the Kent coast, he spotted a V1 near Hastings and, having closed to within 200 yards of the missile, he fired three long bursts that caused the flying bomb to veer right and eventually hit the ground to the northeast of Hastings. This missile was the first of Spencer's seven V1 successes. He survived the war, as did his mount, which was used by other pilots to destroy two more flying bombs.

9

Tempest V JN754/SA-A of Flt Lt H N Sweetman, No 486 Sqn RNZAF, Newchurch, June-July 1944

Flying the mighty Tempest V, Kiwi-manned No 486 Sqn became one of the leading anti-V1 units. Among its successful pilots was 22-year-old Harvey Sweetman, who destroyed his first three missiles in mid-June whilst flying JN754 and was to claim two more of his eventual 11.5 V1s in it. This particular aircraft was also used by other V1 aces, with Flg Off Bill Hart and Plt Off Kevin McCarthy also adding to their scores in JN754. Aside from his V1 successes, Sweetman also made 11 claims, including three destroyed, against aircraft. He later became a test pilot.

10

Spitfire XIV NH714/RWO of Wg Cdr R W Oxspring, No 24 Wing, Lympne, June-July 1944

In March 1944 Bobby Oxspring became the Wing Leader of No 24 Wing and adopted this Griffon-engined Spitfire XIV as his personal mount, which, as was his privilege, carried his initials. He destroyed his first V1 near Redbridge during the early evening of 23 June, sharing its demise with a Tempest V. Over the next four weeks Oxspring destroyed another four flying bombs, with his next victory on 19 July making him a V1 ace. All were claimed when flying NH714, which was notionally on the strength of No 322 (Dutch) Sqn. It later saw

service in Europe with No 350 (Belgian) Sqn, and was eventually sold to the Royal Thai Air Force in 1950.

11

Spitfire XIV RB188/DL-K of Flt Lt H D Johnson, No 91 Sqn, West Malling, June-July 1944

With 13.5 kills to his name, Flt Lt 'Johnny' Johnson was one of the most successful Spitfire pilots of the V1 campaign. Having served with No 91 Sqn since 1942, he claimed his first kill in this aircraft on 23 June when he shared a V1 near Uckfield. The next day he brought down another near Hawkhurst, again in RB188. Just over a week later Johnson downed three more in this machine, which carried the stunning 'nose art' of a naked red-head riding a V1! Other pilots also used RB188 to shoot down three more 'Divers', including the first success for V1 ace Flg Off Ken Collier. The aircraft later served on the Continent with Nos 130 and 350 (Belgian) Sqns, and eventually it too was sold to Thailand.

12

Typhoon IB MN134/SF-S of Flg Off A N Sames, No 137 Sqn, Manston, June-July 1944

By the time of the V1 campaign, Typhoon squadrons were almost exclusively employed on ground support to the Allied armies in Normandy. However, No 137 Sqn was based at Manston, making it ideally placed to use the aircraft's performance against the flying bombs. The unit claimed its first V1 on 22 June, and four days later New Zealander Flg Off 'Artie' Sames, flying MN134, sent a flying bomb crashing into the sea off Bexhill. He then spotted another one over land, which he also destroyed. Sames claimed a third V1 in this aircraft on 14 July, a fourth in MN169 the following day and duly became the only Typhoon V1 ace when he downed his fifth, and last, on 4 August (again in MN169). In total, MN134's pilots destroyed 11.5 V1s, including two by No 137 Sqn's ex-Far East ace Flg Off Henry Nicholls and Manston's Station Commander, Wg Cdr Gordon Raphael, who was a nightfighter ace.

13

Tempest V JN801/SA-L of WO J H Stafford, No 486 Sqn RNZAF, Newchurch, 30 June 1944

Tempest JN801 was a very successful aircraft against V1s, with its pilots bringing down 17 flying bombs and sharing in the destruction of two more. All but one of these victories were claimed by future V1 aces, among them WO 'Jack' Stafford, who achieved his fourth success in it near Robertsbridge during the mid-evening of 30 June. He became a V1 ace on 4 July, eventually taking his total to eight. Stafford later moved with No 486 Sqn onto the Continent, where he was to be credited with five aerial victories, including a share in a Me 262. He survived the war to return to New Zealand, while JN801 later moved to No 222 Sqn and, post-war, became an instructional airframe.

14

Tempest V JN751/RB of Wg Cdr R P Beamont, No 150 Wing, Newchurch, July- August 1944

With 31 flying bombs destroyed, 'Bea' Beamont was the fourth most successful V1 ace. Leading Tempest V-equipped No 150 Wing, he opened his flying bomb 'score' on the first day of the campaign, 16 June, when he shared a V1 with Flt Sgt Bob Cole. Forty-eight hours later he claimed his fifth to become the first V1 ace. In early July JN751 replaced Beamont's previous mount (EJ525), and on the 4th he claimed his first V1 (and 14th overall) in it when he brought a 'Diver' down near Hastings. From then until his final success on 22 August, he claimed all but one of his victims at its controls. The following month, with the threat neutralised, Beamont led No 150 Wing onto the Continent, but he was soon shot down by flak and made a PoW.

15

Tempest V JN812/JF-M of Sqn Ldr A S Dredge, No 3 Sqn Newchurch, June-July 1944

Alan Dredge, who had claimed four victories flying Hurricanes with No 253 Sqn during the Battle of Britain, led No 3 Sqn throughout the V1 campaign, during which it became the most successful anti-V1 squadron. He claimed his first flying bomb shortly before 2100 hrs on 23 June, when he shared in the destruction of a V1 whilst at the controls of this aircraft. Dredge used it again two days later when he claimed his second 'Diver' victory, and he became a V1 ace on the evening of 12 July when his missile was one of 20 destroyed by his squadron that day. On 22 July, again flying JN812, Dredge shot down two flying bombs during separate sorties to claim his last V1s. He left the squadron soon afterwards, but was killed in a flying accident in May 1945. JN812 was shot down over Holland on 1 October 1944.

16

Tempest V EJ527/SA-Q of Flt Sgt O D Eagleson, No 486 Sqn RNZAF, Newchurch, July 1944

With 23 flying bombs destroyed, Flt Sgt 'Ginger' Eagleson was No 486 Sqn's most successful pilot against the V1, whilst the squadron was the second highest scoring unit overall. He had opened his account on 18 June, and within just five days had become a V1 ace. Eagleson's first success when flying this aircraft came on the afternoon of 7 July when he brought down a V1 near No 486 Sqn's temporary base at Newchurch. He was flying it again on 12 July when he shared in the destruction of a 'Diver' intercepted over Dover. A further 3.5 missiles fell to EJ527 whilst it was being flown by V1 aces Flg Off Jimmy Cullen, Flt Lt 'Pip' Powell and WO Sid Short. The aircraft did not last long, however, for it was wrecked in a crash after suffering engine failure on 20 July.

17

Spitfire XIV RB159/DW-D of Sqn Ldr R A Newbery, No 610 'County of Chester' Sqn, Lympne, June-September 1944

'Dickie' Newbery who had eight claims against aircraft, including several destroyed, was in command of No 610 Sqn when it became the first frontline unit to receive the Spitfire XIV. He was allocated RB159 during the summer, and flew it regularly throughout the period of the V1 campaign, during which he personally destroyed eight missiles and shared in the destruction of two more. Newbery achieved all his successes when at its controls, the first two being brought down over the Channel during a mid-morning patrol on 20 June. He claimed his fifth V1 when he shared one over the Channel just after dawn three days later, and his last claim was made on 11 July. Later, Newbery led No 610 Sqn to the Continent, where he ended his lengthy tour. RB159 also had a long career, later serving with Nos 350, 41 and 416 Sqns, before being scrapped in 1949.

18

Spitfire XIV NH654/DL-? of Capitaine J-M Maridor, No 91 Sqn, West Malling, 7 July 1944

Jean-Marie Maridor, a 24-year-old Free French Air Force pilot, enjoyed a successful career with No 91 Sqn. Flying Spitfire XIVs, he was active during the V1 campaign, shooting down his first on 18 June. Maridor destroyed his fifth to become a V1 ace on 5 July, and later that same day he was flying this Spitfire when he shot down his sixth near Canterbury. This proved to be his penultimate success, as he then did not encounter another V1 until 3 August. Seeing it heading towards Benenden School, which was being used as a military hospital, Maridor closed in before opening fire so as to ensure a kill. His aircraft (RM656) was destroyed when the missile exploded, killing him instantly. Unlike the unfortunate Maridor, NH654 survived the war and was later transferred to the Belgian Air Force.

19

Spitfire XIV NH718/3W-G of Flg Off R F Burgwal, No 322 (Dutch) Sqn, West Malling, 8 July 1944

NH718 was one of the more successful individual Spitfire XIVs of the V1 campaign, with its pilots destroying 8.5 missiles whilst at its controls. The first missile to fall to the aircraft was claimed by No 322's South African CO, Maj Keith Kuhlmann, on 23 June. He destroyed another in it in July, as did V1 ace Flg Off Jan Jongbloed, who shot down two. However, it was whilst being flown by No 322 Sqn's top scoring pilot, Flg Off Rudi Burgwal, on 8 July that NH718 made its mark. During a late evening patrol he shot down four missiles and shared in a fifth in less than 40 minutes to become a 'V1 ace in a sortie'. By that time, however, Burgwal already had 7.5 kills to his name, and he was eventually credited with 24 destroyed. Sadly, he was lost over France on a sweep on 12 August. NH718 survived the war, however, and it was later transferred to the Belgian Air Force.

20

Spitfire IX ML242/SK-A of Flt Lt J K Porteous, No 165 Sqn, Lympne, 16 July 1944

New Zealander Flt Lt Jim Porteous was serving as a flight commander in No 165 Sqn when it moved to Kent in June to participate in the anti-V1 campaign. Presentation Spitfire ML242 was the aircraft of squadron CO Sqn Ldr Blackstone, but Porteous flew it on his first anti-'Diver' patrol on the evening of 29 June. He flew twice the next day, and then regularly throughout July, shooting down the third of his six V1s in it on the 16th. By the time the squadron was withdrawn from 'Diver' ops in early August it had been credited with destroying 59.5 V1s, making it the most successful of the Merlin-engined Spitfire units.

21

P-61A Black Widow 42-5547 "BORROWED TIME" of 1Lt H E Ernst and Flt Off E H Kopsel, 422nd NFS, Ford, 16 July 1944

Among the P-61 crews employed on anti-V1 patrols was 2Lt Herman Ernst and his radar operator Flt Off Ed Kopsel, who flew their missions from Ford while on detachment from Scorton. On the evening of 16 July they took off in their usual Black Widow (42-5547), which bore the name "BORROWED TIME" on the nose as well as full D-Day stripes. They were vectored onto a V1, and firing their battery of 20 mm cannon they sent it down into the Channel. This was the 422nd NFS's first combat claim, and Ernst and Kopsel went on to score five night victories over France and Germany during the coming months.

22
Mustang III FB393/UZ-U of Flt Sgt J Zalenski, No 306 (Polish) Sqn, Brenzett, July-August 1944

Flt Sgt Josef Zalenski, who was to claim 9.5 V1s during July and August, shot down his first flying bomb at the controls of this Mustang III near Rye on the afternoon of 16 July. He became a 'Diver' ace 13 days later, and on 30 July was again in FB393 when he shot down his sixth missile. Zalenski's final V1 kill in FB393 came a week later when, early on 7 August, he brought down a 'Diver' over Kent for his eighth success. FB393 was also flown by fellow V1 ace Flt Lt Wlodzimierz Klawe to claim his penultimate success on 23 August. No 306 Sqn was the second highest scoring Polish unit against the V1.

23
Spitfire IX ML117/JX-D of Flg Off D H Davy, No 1 Sqn, Lympne, July 1944

Among the Merlin-engined Spitfire units moved to Kent for 'Diver' operations was No 1 Sqn, which made the first of its 42 claims on 27 June. The unit produced two V1 aces, the second of which was Flg Off 'Dave' Davy, who had previously claimed several victories during 1943. Destroying his first V1 on 4 July, he claimed his next near Ashford during the evening of the 22nd whilst flying ML117. Davy became a V1 ace the very next day when three missiles fell to his guns, and he had his final successes, again in this aircraft, on 26 July when he shot a 'Diver' down off Folkestone and shared in the destruction of a second a short while later. Both Davy and ML117 remained with No 1 Sqn until war's end, the latter eventually becoming an instructional airframe.

24
Mustang III FZ154/PK-N of Flt Lt M Cwynar, No 315 (Polish) Sqn, Brenzett, 22 July 1944

FZ154, unusually for an RAF Mustang III, was fitted with its original framed cockpit rather than the more usual clear Malcolm hood. The fighter was flown throughout much of June by future V1 ace Flt Sgt Tadeusz Jankowski, although it was another pilot, Flt Sgt Kijak, who first claimed a flying bomb with FZ154. During the gloom of late evening on 22 July, the aircraft was being flown by five-victory ace Flt Lt Michal Cwynar when, just north of Ashford, he shot down a V1. Ten minutes later he claimed a second, which, like his earlier kill, was shared with a pilot from another unit. On 24 July Cwynar achieved the distinction of becoming a V1 ace, although he was flying a different Mustang III on this occasion. FZ154 was later transferred to other units and, like Cwynar, survived the war.

25
Typhoon IB MN627/SF-N of Plt Off H T Nicholls, No 137 Sqn, Manston, 31 July 1944

Cornishman Henry Nicholls had become one of the few pilots to become an ace over Malaya in 1942. Having also managed to escape death or capture by the Japanese, he eventually returned to Britain, where he later joined Typhoon-equipped No 137 Sqn. With this unit Nicholls was to shoot down three flying bombs during two sorties at night off the French coast in early July, the second of which he engaged at 2500 ft – 'I attacked with cannon

from astern and it exploded on the sea'. He flew this particular aircraft on a similar, but uneventful, sortie over the Channel before the squadron returned to ground attack duties.

26
Meteor I EE222/YQ-G of Wg Cdr A McDowall, No 616 'South Yorkshire' Sqn, Manston, August 1944

No 616 Sqn gave the RAF's first jet fighter its combat debut during the anti-V1 campaign, the unit being led by Battle of Britain ace Wg Cdr Andrew McDowall, who had previously tested the Meteor with manufacturer Gloster. He adopted Meteor I EE222 as his personal aircraft, the fighter being adorned with his rank pennant. McDowall flew his first anti-V1 patrol in it over the Ashford-Robertsbridge line on the day his squadron began operations – 27 July. He regularly flew EE222 on operations until, when taking off on the afternoon of 29 August, the aircraft suffered a problem and McDowall had to crash land three miles south of Manston. Although he was uninjured, EE222 was badly damaged.

27
Mosquito XIX TA400/VY-J of Flg Off A J Owen and Flg Off S V McAllister, No 85 Sqn, West Malling, 4/5 August 1944

Mosquito-equipped No 85 Sqn enjoyed considerable success against the V1, with its crews claiming 39.5 missiles destroyed. Among those that downed a V1 was 'Ginger' Owen, who had claimed six victories whilst flying Beaufighters in the Mediterranean. In the summer of 1944 he joined No 85 Sqn and immediately began anti-V1 patrols. In the early hours of 5 August, when flying this aircraft with his long-term radar operator, Flg Off McAllister, he spotted a V1. Diving from 9000 ft, he fired a short burst and sent it crashing near Tenterden. This proved to be Owen's only V1 kill, although other crews claimed a further four missiles in TA400, including two credited to future ace Flt Lt Richard Goucher and his radar operator Flt Lt C H Bullock.

28
Mosquito XVII HK249/RX-B of Sqn Ldr G L Howitt, No 456 Sqn RAAF, Ford, July-August 1944

By the time Geoffrey Howitt joined Australian-manned No 456 Sqn as a flight commander in the spring of 1944, he already had six victories to his name. During the summer he flew HK249 as his regular aircraft, claiming a He 177 probably destroyed in it during mid-June. He was also flying the fighter with his radar operator Flt Lt George Irvine when, shortly after 2300 hrs on 8 August, they attacked a V1 over land at an altitude of about 1000 ft and shot it down. Four nights later the pair, again in this aircraft, attacked another flying bomb from dead astern and caused it to explode in mid-air. To identify its Australian ownership HK249 carried a 'wallaby' roundel on the entrance door. Like its crew, the fighter survived the war.

29
Tempest V EJ644/JJ-G of Wg Cdr J F Fraser, No 274 Sqn, West Malling and Manston, 16/17 August 1944

During July and August 1944 Wg Cdr Joe Fraser, who had become an ace flying Gladiators in Greece during 1941, was attached as a supernumerary pilot to No 274 Sqn, with whom he regularly participated in operations. He flew his first 'anti-"Diver"' patrol on 8 August, and seven days later was forced to break off an attack due to the balloon barrage. Fraser flew his first 'Diver' sortie in this aircraft on 16 August, when he fired three bursts at a V1 and noted 'hits only'. However, he had better luck the following morning during a 75-minute sortie when (again in EJ644) he shot down a flying bomb to the east of West Malling, which proved to be his final air combat claim.

30

Mustang III FB125/DV-F of Flg Off J Hartley, No 129 Sqn, Brenzett, 19 August 1944

FB125 may well qualify as one of the longest serving Merlin-engined Mustangs, as it flew with No 129 Sqn from April 1944 to April 1945 – an extraordinarily long period for a fighter in World War 2. During the anti-'Diver' campaign its pilots shot down four flying bombs, and it was also flown by several V1 aces. One was Plt Off E W Edwards, who claimed the second of his six successes in it on 16 July. The following month, on 19 August, Flg Off Jim Hartley was at the controls of FB125 off Boulogne when he intercepted a 'Diver' and shot off its starboard wing, causing it to crash into the sea off Dymchurch. This was his eighth flying bomb kill of an eventual total of 12, making him the most successful Mustang III V1 ace.

31

Mustang III HB849/PK-M of Flt Lt J Schmidt, No 315 Sqn, Brenzett, 20 August 1944

Twenty-eight-year-old Jerzy Schmidt made all six of his air combat claims, which included four V1s, during a two-month period in the summer of 1944. He shared in the destruction of two V1s over the Sussex coast in the late morning of 3 August to claim his first 'Diver' success. Shortly before 0800 hrs on the 20th, Schmidt was flying this aircraft over the Kent coast in the New Romney area when he intercepted and shot down a V1, followed by a second ten minutes later. Frustratingly for him, he never had the opportunity to claim his fifth one! Schmidt later became a flight commander, and like HB849 he was lost during an escort mission to Norway in December.

32

Tempest V EJ555/SD-Y of Flt Lt R L T Robb, No 501 'County of Gloucester' Sqn, Bradwell Bay, 25/26 October 1944

On 10 August 1944 the Tempest Flight of the FIU, which had been developing night interception procedures, was renumbered as No 501 Sqn. By October the V1 campaign against Britain was largely reduced to air-launched missiles being fired at Britain from He 111 bombers. It was one such missile that Flt Lt 'Jackson' Robb intercepted in EJ555 on the night of 15 October, the V1 ace shooting it down as it came in over the east coast. This proved to be his 13th, and last, success against the flying bomb menace. The aircraft was used a few nights later by Flg Off Jimmie Grottick to shoot down his first V1. EJ555 left No 501 Sqn in late April 1945 and was eventually scrapped in 1950.

33

Beaufighter VIF V8565/ZQ-F of Flt Lt J H Howard-Williams, FIDS, Coltishall, 4 November 1944

Jeremy Howard-Williams was an experienced nightfighter pilot in the FIU, or FIDS as it had become by late 1944, and as such he did much development work in night interception techniques, including against the low and slow-flying He 111

flying bomb carriers. To that end the FIDS had several Beaufighter VIs on strength due to their better slow-speed handling in comparison with the higher performance Mosquitoes that equipped frontline nightfighter units. Thus it was that he was flying this aircraft, with navigator Flg Off MacRae, on the evening of 4 November when they were vectored onto a missile-carrying He 111 45 miles east of Winterton on a cloudless, hazy autumn evening – the Heinkel had 'popped up' to 1500 ft for the launch. By lowering 30 degrees of flap, Howard-Williams managed to position himself astern and open fire. The bomber, which was quickly shot down, was one of five He 111s lost by II./KG 53 that night.

34

Mosquito XIII MM446/ZJ-Y of Wg Cdr E D Crew, No 96 Sqn, Odiham, 15 November 1944

With 21 V1s to his name, as well as 13 victories against aircraft, Edward Crew was one of the RAF's leading nightfighter pilots. He was the second most successful Mosquito pilot against V1s, and with 189 victories his squadron was by some measure the most successful. After the main campaign was over No 96 Sqn resumed more conventional night patrols, including countering the missile-carrying He 111s. MM446 was Crew's allocated aircraft, and it was flown by him on one such sortie on 15 November, which proved to be uneventful. No 96 Sqn disbanded soon afterwards, but Edward Crew went on to have a very distinguished career, eventually rising to become an air vice marshal.

35

Tempest V EJ608/SD-P of Sqn Ldr A Parker-Rees, No 501 'County of Gloucester' Sqn, Bradwell Bay, 5 December 1944

Alastair Parker-Rees had a successful career flying Mosquitoes during the 'Baby Blitz' of early 1944, when he had been credited with three destroyed and two probables. During the V1 campaign he went on to claim eight 'Divers', and in October he became the CO of No 501 Sqn after Sqn Ldr Joe Berry had been killed in action. Under Parker-Rees' leadership the unit continued to perform its hazardous night anti-V1 patrols over eastern England, intercepting missiles launched over the North Sea. It was whilst flying this aircraft on the night of 5 December that he shot down one of the 15 V1s launched against England that day – his unit claimed three missiles in total. This was Parker-Rees' final claim, although EJ608 brought down another 'Diver' later in the month whilst being flown by Flt Lt Lilwal.

36

Mustang III HB861/UZ-B of Flt Lt J Jeka, No 306 (Polish) Sqn, Andrews Field, 6 March 1945

One of the last V1s to fall was claimed by Polish ace Jozef Jeka who, on 21 May 1944, had been shot down but managed to evade capture and return to Britain four months later. Subsequently joining No 306 Sqn and later becoming a flight commander, Jeka flew on escort operations with the unit into the spring of 1945. It was during one such mission that he encountered a V1 over the Continent and shot it down to claim his only 'Diver' kill. His aircraft was adorned with a stylish piece of nose art that would have been more at home on a USAAF Mustang, rather than an RAF one!

Bates, H E, *Flying Bombs over England.* Froglets, 1994

Bennett, John, *Fighter Nights (No 456 Sqn).*
Banner Books,1995

Blake, Steve, *Pioneer Mustang Group (354th FG).*
Schiffer, 2008

Bowyer, Michael, *Fighting Colours.* PSL, 1969 and 1975

Brookes, Andrew, *Fighter Squadron At War (No 85 Sqn).*
Ian Allan, 1980

Cull, Brian, *Diver, Diver, Diver.* Grub St, 2008

Flintham, Vic and Thomas, Andrew, *Combat Codes.*
Airlife, 2003 and 2008

Griffin, John and Kostenuk, Samuel, *RCAF Squadron
Histories and Aircraft.* Stevens, 1977

Halley, James, *Squadrons of the RAF and Commonwealth.*
Air Britain, 1988

Herrington, John, *Australians in the War 1939-45, Series 3
Volume 3.* Halstead Press, 1962

Hess, William, *Osprey Aviation Elite Units 7 – 354th Fighter
Group.* Osprey Publishing, 2002

Hunt, Leslie, *Twenty One Squadrons.* Garnstone Press, 1972

Jefford, Wg Cdr C G, *RAF Squadrons.* Airlife, 1988 and 2001

Kitching T W, *From Dusk till Dawn (No 219 Sqn).* FPD Services,
2001

Milberry, Larry and Halliday, Hugh, *The RCAF at War
1939-1945.* CANAV Books, 1990

Ogley, Bob, *Doodlebugs and Rockets.* Froglets, 1992

Oxspring, Grp Capt Bobby, *Spitfire Command.*
William Kimber, 1984

Rawlings, John D R, *Fighter Squadrons of the RAF.*
Macdonald, 1969

Richards, Denis, *RAF Official History 1939-45, Parts 2 and 3.*
HMSO, 1954

Robertson, Bruce, *Spitfire – The story of a Famous Fighter.*
Harleyford, 1960

Shores, Christopher, *Those Other Eagles.* Grub St, 2004

Shores, Christopher and Williams, Clive, *Aces High Volumes
1 and 2.* Grub St, 1994 and 1999

Sortehaug, Paul, *The Wild Winds (No 486 Sqn).*
Otago University Print, 1998

Terbeck, Helmut, van der Meer, Harry and Sturtivant, Ray,
Spitfire International. Air Britain, 2002

Thomas, Chris and Shores, Christopher, *The Typhoon and
Tempest Story.* Arms & Armour Press, 1988

Thompson, Warren, *Osprey Combat Aircraft 8 – P-61 Black
Widow Units of World War 2.* Osprey Publishing, 1998

ACKNOWLEDGEMENTS
The author wishes to record his gratitude to the following who
have given of their time in presenting accounts or information
for inclusion within this volume – Wg Cdr A D McN Boyd DSO
DFC, the late Flt Lt K G Brain DFC, Wg Cdr B A Burbridge DSO
DFC, the late AVM E D Crew CB DSO DFC, the late AVM L W
G Gill DSO, the late D H Greaves DFC, the late Sqn Ldr J N
Howard-Williams DFC, Sqn Ldr A S Murkowski and Flt Lt P R
Rudd DFC

INDEX